Zephyr's

Tale

A Poodle's Guide To The Behavior Of
Dogs

Con Slobodchikoff

Animal Communications Ltd

This book is an updated version of a previously published book titled Autobiography of a Poodle.

Cover Design by Vila Design

ISBN: 979-8-9897182-0-7 (E-Book)

ISBN: 979-8-9897182-1-4 (Print Book)

CONTENTS

My Name Is Zephyr

I 'm a lucky dog. I could have been out roaming the streets, hungry, sick, and lonely. Or, I could have been one of the many dogs locked behind fences, ignored and forgotten. Instead, I have two wonderful humans who love me, a nice house to live in, and great places to go for walks. I've run through meadows, danced in the rain and the snow, and explored the depths of the human-dog bond with insatiable curiosity. I just wish all dogs could live like me.

*Here I am as a puppy, with my
person Con.*

In these pages, I invite you to join me on a journey through the looking glass of my life. My name is Zephyr, and I'm an apricot Standard Poodle. My people are Con and Judy, and I have to share them with a cat called Seri and another Standard Poodle called Raja. Seri is a gray-and-white tabby that Con and Judy brought home from the Humane Society. She's several years older than I am, and just because she can open doors and jump up on tall pieces of furniture, she thinks that cats are smarter than dogs. I, of course, disagree. Raja is a black dog who came into my life several years after I moved in with Con and Judy.

Let me tell you my story. I was born in a kennel in central California, where people breed Standard Poodles. I had two brothers and three sisters, and in the first few weeks of my life, I enjoyed cuddling with them. Even before my eyes opened, I liked the warmth and security of being in a mass of squirmy puppies. As we all got older and looked out at the world around us, we started taking tentative steps and wandering away from our mom, starting to push the limits of our daring and independence. We also started playing with one another, both for fun and for the practice of testing who was going to be more dominant than whom.

These first few weeks are crucial to a dog's proper development. Without this period of socialization, puppies who are taken away from their dog families too early never really get to know how to relate to other dogs and become social and emotional cripples for the rest of their lives. Fortunately, the people in the kennel knew this and let us grow up as puppies in our dog family for about eight weeks before they were willing to consider selling us. During these first eight weeks, we had the opportunity to learn all the doggish protocols we would need to meet and interact with dogs later on when we were adults. And, at eight weeks, we were ready to start learning about the other species that would loom large in our lives: humans.

When I was seven weeks old, my dog mom explained many of the facts of life to me – my mission in life was to find some kindly and nice humans to take good care of me. Mind you, this would not be a one-sided street. By being nice to my humans, I would bring warmth and comfort into their lives. I would give them unconditional Love, what all humans need and search for, a search that usually ends in dismal failure until they find the dog of their dreams.

Finding the dog of your dreams is not easy, let me tell you. It requires hard work on our part and often gets derailed by people who choose the wrong dog despite all of our efforts at matchmaking. As my dog mom told me, I would know when the right people came to get me. Then I should try as hard as possible to convince them to take me home.

You know, it happened! My future human dad and mom, Con and Judy, walked in with the idea of just looking at the puppies in my litter. They weren't planning on taking a puppy home because although Con wanted a dog, Judy wasn't sure she wanted one. They already had Seri, the cat, living at home with them, and Judy thought that a cat was a perfect companion. Dogs were messy, loud, demanded attention. Cats were clean, quiet, and independent.

So, when I was brought into the room where Con and Judy were waiting, I quickly realized that Judy was the one who needed to be convinced. I concentrated on her. I played with her, I cuddled up to her, I let myself be picked up, I tried to lick her, I finally curled up right next to her. Con I ignored, for I knew that he was already converted.

Judy was charmed. Her defenses were down, and she found it very touching that I trusted her enough to curl up and sleep beside her. The moment happened, just like my dog mom told me! Judy turned to Con and said, "Shall we buy this puppy?"

Con quickly agreed, the papers were signed, and they belonged to me!

They didn't take me home right away, because they had come to California to spend a weekend in Carmel. Little did they know that they would spend the next two days browsing through bookstores, looking for an appropriate name. They wanted something sort of dignified to suit me when I was a grown-up, elegant Standard Poodle. But they also wanted to be able to shorten it into a nickname without it sounding dumb. And it had to have some sort of hard consonant sound in it, so that I would be able to hear it from a distance and come running, even on a windy day.

Judy was the one who came across the name in, of all things, a what-to-name-your-baby book.

"Zephyr!" Judy said. "How do you like the name Zephyr? It means 'gentle wind from the West'."

"Yes, yes!" said Con. "That sounds just right! And we can shorten it to Zeph."

When they came to pick me up for the long ride to my new home, they tried out my new name on me. I liked it. It wasn't too cutesy or tough or embarrassing. I could hold my head up high around other dogs or around other humans when my people called out "Zephyr!" But in the long run, it really didn't matter to me what they called me, as much as it mattered how they called me. As long as they were going to speak that name with affection, I would come to recognize it and would respond to it instantly.

As the car turned east toward my new home, reality finally dawned on Judy. She started to scream.

"We bought a dog, oh my God, we bought a dog! Whatever possessed us to do that! How could we have bought a dog? How did that happen?" she kept repeating.

I could have told her. She and Con were the right people for me, so everything clicked into place without a hitch. It was that simple.

Puppy Stuff

The trip back to Con and Judy's house was long. I had never ridden in a car before, and suddenly there I was, in a cardboard box on the back seat, rolling and lurching with every bump. Fortunately, I didn't get carsick, the way some dogs can when they're not used to riding in cars.

Judy thought that I would be too frightened if I were left by myself, so she and Con alternated between driving and sitting in the back seat to keep me company. The swaying of the car made me sleepy, and I slept much of the way. The rest of the time I was missing my littermates, my mom, and my former house. Even though I was sure that Con and Judy were the right people, I couldn't help worrying about what was going to happen to me.

While I was lightly dozing, I could hear Con and Judy talking about the kinds of things that they would have to buy.

"Toys," Judy said. "We don't have any toys for him."

"Let's make a list," Con said. "What do we need?"

"To start," said Judy, "we need some dishes. We'll need a food dish and a water dish. We need a flat buckle collar, so that he'll get used to wearing something around his neck, and a leash."

"Right," said Con, "and we need a pooper-scooper and some plastic bags, preferably the kind that zip together across the top when we put in his poop."

"So that brings us back to toys," said Judy.

"Well," said Con, "one thing we know is that we can't let him play with old towels, sweaters, shoes, or anything else that he can chew. Puppies can't tell the difference between an old shoe and a set of expensive dress shoes that you have to wear tomorrow."

"So what does that leave us?"

"Well," said Con, "another thing we know is that we don't want the squeaky kinds of toys that have a whistle built into them. It would be too easy for him to chew out the whistle and swallow it. And, speaking of swallowing, we don't want anything that is small enough for him to swallow. A dog can die from swallowing a toy that gets stuck in its stomach.

"So what does that leave us?" asked Judy again, getting slightly dismayed with the list of things that I shouldn't have as toys.

"I understand that nylon bones are pretty good for puppies to chew on, as long as the bones are too big to swallow. And toys made out of shearling, such as soft Frisbees, are good for games of catch or fetch. We'll have to make sure that he knows that he can play with his toys, but that he can't chew on anything else."

"And how do we do that?"

"We watch him all the time, and the second he starts chewing on something else, we gently grab his muzzle, give it a small squeeze, and say No! firmly."

"What about if he starts chewing on our hands or fingers?"

"Same thing. Gently squeeze his muzzle and say No!"

At that point, I drifted into a deep sleep and thought that I was back with my littermates, happily romping around the yard.

"Zephyr, wake up!" I heard Judy say. "It's time for you to stretch your legs."

Con and Judy had stopped in the parking lot of a large store, well away from other people and other dogs. They were concerned about me since I didn't have all of my shots yet, and the breeder had cautioned them about the dangers of infection from parvo or other diseases. I would later find that this cautious approach toward disease would keep me away from other dogs for about another month until I had had most of my shots.

And so we traveled for what seemed like forever, with me sleeping most of the time and then occasionally having a few minutes out of the car in the back part of some parking lot. I thought the trip would never end.

Finally, however, the trip did end. We had arrived at Con and Judy's house, my new home. I was eager to see it, to see if it lived up to my expectations.

Con and Judy had not expected to come home with a dog, so they had not puppy-proofed their house.

When we rolled into the garage, Con said, "Judy, stay with Zephyr in the car while I go up and check the house to make sure that there isn't anything around that can hurt him."

Naturally, I didn't think that there could have been anything that could hurt me.

Much as I hate to admit it, I was wrong – the typical house has a lot of stuff in it that could hurt a puppy. Some things are obvious, like electrical cords. Puppies like to chew on things, and chewing on an electrical cord can be a nasty experience. Other things are not so obvious, like some houseplants that can end a dog's life practically as quickly as an electrical cord.

But I was tired, and I was bored with sitting in a car. I wanted to see my new house, and I was impatient to get on with it!

Con ran up the stairs and disappeared, while Judy tried to quiet my whines.

"It's all right, Zephyr, we just don't want you to hurt yourself," she kept repeating.

Con looked around the house. Electrical cords were everywhere. Houseplants were all over the place. Con knew that the houseplants were safe. From the time that he and Judy adopted Seri, he had made sure that all the plants that were in the house were not poisonous to animals. But cats aren't big chewers the way young puppies are, and so neither Con nor Judy was concerned with Seri chewing anything other than an occasional non-poisonous houseplant.

A quick check showed that the house was almost puppy-proof. All the cleansers were properly stored in cabinets, out of reach of an inquisitive puppy. The garbage was securely packed in a plastic container with a tight lid that wouldn't open even if the container were knocked down. Con ran around stuffing electrical cords behind items of furniture and picking up random items of clothing, socks, shoes, pens, pencils, coins, glasses, and medicine containers that were scattered around the house within a puppy's reach.

At last, Con came down to the garage and said, "OK, Zephyr, welcome to your new home!"

My New House

My new house.

The house was strange and difficult. Con and Judy carried me up some stairs leading from the garage to the main part of the house and plopped me down in the living room. Naturally, I started to explore. Part of the living room seemed to consist of enormous windows, from floor to ceiling, looking out on some trees. The furniture was pretty sparse, so it was relatively easy for me to look across the entire room. Everything seemed big compared to my kennel back home. I felt like a small, insignificant creature standing in the middle of the floor.

The living room had carpet, so I could walk around without a problem, but when I wandered into the kitchen on its parquet floor, my legs splayed out, and down I went. There were stairs going up to a second story where Con and Judy's bedroom was, and I was expected to go up those stairs to get to a deck on the back side of the house. That would take me down some other stairs to my pen outside. Up and down, down and up, and I was rather unsteady on my feet in a straight stretch, much less going up and down stairs.

The first thing Con and Judy wanted me to do was meet Seri the cat. They wanted desperately for us to get along, to become lifelong friends, and to share a happy and peaceful existence. Both felt somewhat guilty. Here, Seri, up to now, had had all of the attention, and suddenly, someone else was going to compete for strokes. If things didn't go well, both Con and Judy would feel terrible – in one blow, they ruined the life of their much-adored cat, and who knows how this new dog would work out?

Seri was a shy cat. She would hide when people would come over to visit. She didn't like to meet anyone new. She loved being the center of attention, as long as the attention came from her two humans. Otherwise, she put no trust in the world around her. Con and Judy thought that Seri probably had been abused by someone when she was a kitten, and from an early age she had no confidence that people in general were worth knowing. Some of Seri's behavior clearly suggested that someone had not been kind to her: whenever Con got out the vacuum cleaner, Seri would panic and disappear in a flash, even before Con turned on the machine with its annoying high-pitched whine.

Con brought Seri into the living room to meet me. I saw him holding a small gray cat with black stripes on her tail and yellow-green eyes that were rapidly turning black from the expanding pupils.

Judy waited anxiously.

As soon as Seri saw me, her heart began to race, her ears went back, her tail started to lash, and she tried to jump out of Con's arms.

When she got close to me, she couldn't stand it anymore.

"Meeoowh," she yelled, get me out of here!

With a huge lunge, she jumped out of Con's arms and ran for the kitchen.

Now let me tell you, I'm a poodle, bred originally for hunting. When something in front of me runs, I'm hard-wired to follow. Instinct, it's called. Some things will cause the pre-programmed brain to click in without any prior experience, and for hunting dogs, the sight of a running animal is one of them.

Some people think that dogs are ruled primarily by instincts, while humans have rational minds and are not affected by pre-programmed hard wiring in their brains. If you believe that, ask yourself the next time you see an advertisement in a magazine for a new automobile: why is that young, pretty woman (or, not to be sexist about it, that young, handsome man) standing next to the automobile? Why not an old man of ninety-five, standing with a cane and a crutch? After all, the old man could probably use the car more than a young person, who could walk or take the bus. Obviously, you silly dog, you answer, it is done to sell cars. And why do pretty young people, who have nothing to do with cars, sell cars? Could it be that some pre-programmed hard-wired routine kicks in, providing an association of pleasure between the car and the pretty person?

But I digress. Seri ran for the kitchen, and I ran after her, and Con and Judy ran after me. Seri hit the polished parquet floor and started to skid. I hit the polished parquet floor, and all four legs went in different directions. Suddenly, I was a ten-pound missile, completely out of control. Seri slowed down slightly to jump up on the kitchen counter, where she knew that she would be safe. At that point, I slid into her, and together we slid into the wall, a tangle of feet and tails. Ah, togetherness, a great way to start a new friendship!

As Con ran into the room, Seri jumped free, jumped up on the counter, and then jumped up on top of a kitchen cabinet that rose almost up to the ceiling. There she stayed. Con and Judy tried to coax her down, but she had had enough for one evening. Whatever this clumsy creature was (she suspected even then that I was a dog), she wanted nothing to do with me. And, by extension, since Con and Judy brought me into her house, she wanted nothing to do with them, either.

Judy was upset.

"I knew it," she said. "She'll never forgive us. We have torn up her life, and nothing will ever be the same again."

Con tried to be reassuring.

"It's going to take a little time, but they'll be fine. Just wait, they'll be great friends. You'll see."

Forget it, was Seri's attitude. This is my house. Take that creature and get out! All of you! And by the way, please come back every day to feed and stroke me. Otherwise, I don't want to have anything to do with any of you! Out, out, out!

The things that people heap on a dog! Not only did I have to learn my way around this up-and-down house, but now I had to make my peace with a cat who apparently hated my guts from the very second she saw me.

I saw that life had thrown me a curve. I thought that I would have sole ownership of my people, to bend them around my paw and have them cater to my every wish. Now I saw that I would have to share my people with another animal. Worse yet, the other animal was a cat!

Living with a Cat

*Seri avoiding Zephyr by jump-
ing on a counter.*

After several days of Seri avoiding me, the question of the day was, how do you get a dog and a cat to make friends? Con and Judy thought long and hard about that.

"I know!" Con finally said. "I'll take Seri in my arms, hold her tight, and we'll bring Zephyr over to her and let them sniff each other. When they get the smell of each other, they'll get the idea that they both belong here."

"Well, I guess it's worth trying," said Judy, somewhat reluctantly.

Con caught Seri, cuddled her in his arms, and brought her over to me to smell.

Even if she was a cat, I was willing to try to be accommodating. After all, I was going to live with her, so I thought I might as well make the best of the situation.

No one told me, however, about cat protocols. I didn't realize that there were certain conventions that had to be followed with a cat. Now I know that first you have to approach slowly and let the cat smell you, then you have to make gentle contact with the cat's mouth or chest. After that, if you smell nice, there is a slim chance that the cat might accept you as worthy of affection.

But I'm an enthusiastic dog, and dogs don't do that sort of thing. We just wade into the fray, sticking our wet noses first at another dog's nose, then at more distant parts toward the back end. If you are a dominant dog, you just poke your nose right in, letting the chips fall where they may.

So I stuck my wet nose into Seri's face, took a big sniff, then moved my nose toward her tail, leaving gobs of drool all over her body.

Seri was not impressed. Her eyes dilated, her ears rotated backward, and she started to growl and wiggle in Con's arms.

"I don't think it's working," said Judy.

"Hold Zephyr by the collar for a moment, while I get a better grip on Seri," said Con.

Seri meanwhile had wiggled out a paw, and before I knew what happened, she swiped the paw and her claws across my nose.

Take that, you ugly dog, and besides, you smell bad! Seri said. Get out of my face! And while you're at it, get out of my house!

My nose started to hurt, and I yelped. Get me out of here, I thought. I ran to Judy and hid behind her legs.

"Con, Zephyr's hurt!" yelled Judy.

"Seri, hold still!" yelled Con.

"Groowll, meowww" yelled Seri.

I was too stunned to yell.

Seri decided that she had enough for the day. She squirmed out of Con's arms, ran up his shoulder, dug her hind claws into his neck, and used him as a launching pad to leap across the room and disappear up the stairs.

"Aooww!" yelled Con.

"What do we do now?" yelled Judy.

"I guess we keep trying," said Con, wiping blood from his neck.

As beginnings go, it wasn't the best. I look back to that time now and wonder what we all might have done differently. Con tells me that when a person brings a newly adopted cat into a house for a resident cat to meet, the best thing to do is to put them into separate rooms with the door closed and let them get used to each other's smell. Then the door can be opened just a little bit, not enough for each of them to squeeze through, but enough for them to sniff noses. After perhaps several weeks of this procedure, the door can be opened and the two cats can finally mingle with each other. Even then, they might both sit and stare at each other through the doorway for hours or days, working out their dominance protocols. Certainly, they wouldn't just rush in and start smelling each other's bottoms the way two dogs would do.

Maybe it would have been best to just let Seri get used to my smell, and have her come up to me when she was ready. Unfortunately for that idea, Seri is a very shy cat, and she probably would never have come up to me. Shyness is not one of my virtues. I would have always charged up to her, all four feet flying.

Anyway, the first step was taken. Seri now knew that Con and Judy were serious about keeping me around and that they wanted us to be friends. She still wanted no part of anything to do with me, however.

After a couple of weeks together, we worked out a routine. Seri would carefully inspect the hallways to see if I was around, then run as fast as she could toward her food dish or her litter box. When I saw her run, I would immediately chase her. If I got close, she would jump up on anything that was handy – a chair, a sofa, a table – flatten her ears and growl. If I got too close, which I usually did, she would swipe at my nose with her claws. I learned very quickly to be alert and avoid her paw.

This went on for months. I tried reasoning with her, but her opinion of me and my manners was about the same as the opinion of the anthropologist who was invited out to dinner by a bunch of cannibals. For a while, I thought that Seri was convinced that I would kill and eat her if I could only catch her.

Con and Judy took this all quite seriously. They both tried to keep me from chasing her every time I ran after her. Somewhat unfairly, they seemed to think that Seri was defending herself when she swiped at my nose and never yelled at her. Con would catch me, put his face close to my nose, and say sternly, "Don't chase Seri!" I was hurt that he never grabbed Seri and never yelled "Don't slice up Zephyr!"

Gradually, things settled down. Seeing that she was still alive after months of coexistence, Seri started accepting me. She still jumped up on things and swiped at my nose when she saw me coming, but the claws were sheathed, and the growl was half-hearted.

Eventually, it became more of an act than a reality. Seri would look frightened, and make Con and Judy feel guilty about inflicting a dog on her life, but she really enjoyed the interactions. If nothing else, it gave her something to do, besides watching the birds outside the windows and soliciting strokes from Con and Judy.

Seri even started toying with me. She would make sure that Con or Judy was nearby, then run past me. Naturally, I would chase after her, my instinct to chase after a running animal kicking in at that point. Con or Judy would then start saying, "Don't chase Seri!" and would grab me, telling me "No! Bad dog!" Seri, meanwhile, would be laughing on the sidelines, because she knew that neither one realized that she was just playing with me and my chasing instinct.

Finally, Con realized that Seri was putting on an act. The great day came when Con decided to take both of us, Seri and me, on a car ride. Riding in cars is one of Seri's great pleasures. She loves watching the other cars, the birds, the people. She particularly loves riding in a car at night in areas that are lit up with bright neon lights.

Con thought that having us both in the car might make Seri a little less nervous about me. He loaded an excited me, a very nervous Judy, and an apparently nervous Seri into the car, and off we went. Judy was holding me in her lap and was also holding me by a leash, in case I got crazed and attacked Seri. As always, Seri was free to roam inside the car.

Seri was so excited about being out on a drive that she forgot to pretend that she was terrified of me. She roamed past my nose, looking out the window and purring. She practically stepped on me, moving from the front dashboard to the side windows.

"Looks like Seri isn't that afraid of Zephyr," said Con.

"Guess not," said Judy.

Not at all, said Zephyr.

How to Train a Dog

Almost as soon as I got settled into my new home, Con and Judy decided that I needed training. I didn't think so, at all. After all, I was just a little over eight weeks old, and I was prepared for a long puppyhood. Training just didn't figure into it in the least. If human children get to be kids up until the age of twenty-five or thirty, surely dogs can be puppies for a few years.

Con and Judy had other ideas. They thought that the earlier I learned such words as "sit," "come," "down," "heel," and "stay," the easier I would be to live with.

Fortunately, they believed in positive reward training. I just cannot believe how many people think that the best way to get a dog to do something is to bully it, coerce it, or generally make its life unpleasant.

Somebody who is an alleged expert says, "The proper way to control a dog is to take a choke-chain, and give the dog a hard yank. If the dog doesn't obey instantly, pull the leash over a branch or door, and let the dog hang suspended for a while. That'll show him who is boss. Or, if that fails, hit the dog over the head with a stick."

So when was the last time you cheerfully did what your boss wanted you to do, after he or she suspended you from a door frame for a few minutes, allowing you to hang by the neck until your breath started to leave you? Or hit you over the head with a stick every time you looked puzzled because the simpleton couldn't clearly convey to you what he or she wanted and expected?

Sure, someone engaging in such behavior is to be feared. Who knows when they will go off the deep end again? But obeyed willingly? Hardly. Loved? Hardly. Respected? Not likely. Dogs are not surrogates for people to express their violent urges.

Positive reward training is both fun and helps build a stronger bond between dog and person. The method is so simple that most people can grasp it relatively quickly, without having to take courses in Learning Theory at the local college.

"Come on, Zephyr," said Judy, "we are going to start with your training."

They brought me into the living room and plopped me down on the rug. What next, I wondered?

Suddenly, I smelled a delicious smell, that later I learned was fake bacon. It smelled so wonderful, I just wanted to smell it forever. Saliva filled my mouth. Even though I didn't know what it was, I just knew it had to have a wonderful taste.

Judy brought her hand next to my nose. There was the smell! It was coming from her hand! She had something in her hand that was simply wonderful! I wanted it! I needed it! I had to have it! I would do anything for it!

Oops. I did do anything for it. As I stood there, Judy brought her hand past my nose, up over the back of my head, and said, "Sit!"

I lifted up my nose and my head to get at this wonderful smell, lost my balance, and sat down on my haunches.

"Good boy! Good boy! Zephyr is a good boy!" said Judy in a high, sing-song voice, giving me the object in her hand and patting my head.

Oh, wonderful food! It tasted as good as it smelled. The only problem was, there was only a small morsel, enough to tease the tongue but nowhere near enough to fill the belly. I wanted more!

Judy's hand came near my nose again, with another piece of food.

"Down," she said, bringing her hand all the way down to the floor.

My nose followed. I reached for the food, but the only way that I could get my nose close enough was to push out my front feet and lie down on the rug.

"Good boy! Good boy! Zephyr is a good boy!" said Judy in a high, sing-song voice again. And once again I tasted that delicious morsel.

Then I got carried away. I could still smell the food on Judy's hand, so I reached over and gently bit her hand.

"No! Naah!" said Judy in a low, growling voice.

I retreated from her hand, realizing I had overstepped my bounds. In the dog world, low-pitched growls mean a threat that you are in some danger of being bitten or disciplined if the growl comes from your dog mom. High-pitched whines are what you get from your friendly litter mates when they are playing with you, or what you get from your dog mom when she is particularly pleased with you. We respond to high-pitched voices with pleasure, and to low-pitched voices with caution.

I continued to remain lying down, now looking abashed and contrite.

Judy brought her hand up over my head again, with another morsel of food, and said, "Sit!" I reached my nose up, but couldn't quite reach the food, so I sat up on my haunches.

"Good boy! Good boy! Zephyr is a good boy!" Again the same high-pitched voice, again the delicious morsel of food.

Judy brought her hand down again, with another piece of food, and kept her hand about a foot from my nose.

"Zephyr, Heel!" she said, walking forward slowly.

I started to walk forward, following the smell and the hand.

"Zephyr, Heel!" she said again, continuing to walk forward, with the hand held about a foot from my nose at face-height as I was walking forward. And so we walked around the living room, with Judy periodically saying "Zephyr, Heel!" Finally, Judy stopped and let me come up to her hand.

She opened up her hand, and as I was eating the tiny scrap of food she had in there, she patted me on the head, and once again repeated in her high-pitched voice, "Good boy! Good boy! Zephyr is a good boy!"

I was very pleased. I getting some delicious smells and superb tastes, and I was being praised in a form of dog-talk that we instinctively appreciate.

Con and Judy were very pleased, also. Not only had I performed well, but I had also gone through three commands (sit, down, and heel) in ten minutes. I got rewarded by the food and the praise, and they got rewarded by watching me do just what they thought I was supposed to do. A happy time was had by all.

Con told me later that a current fashion in dog training is to talk about "cues" instead of "commands." The idea seems to be that the word "command" implies that there will be punishment if the command is not obeyed, while "cue" is more about providing information to the dog to do something.

In his lecturing tone of voice, Con explained that "cue" in animal behavior terms stands for anything that gives an animal meaningful information, and while using the word "cue" for "sit" might be appropriate once I learned what "sit" meant, it was not an appropriate word to use when I had no idea of the concept of "sit." Frankly, I couldn't have cared less. As long as I was given either a food reward or praise for doing something that I was asked to do, I didn't care what people wanted to call it.

Over the course of the next few weeks, such training sessions were a daily occurrence. Every time, the session went exactly the same way. Exactly the same words were used. Exactly the same movements were done. Exactly the same tone of voice was used: high-pitched for praise, low-pitched for correction. No one slapped me, no one pulled a chain around my throat, no one tried to bully me into submission. It was a fun time, and I completely forgot about being resentful for giving up my carefree, undisciplined puppyhood for those ten or fifteen minutes a day that we trained.

Con and Judy made it easier for me to learn by being consistent. By doing everything the same with me, they made it possible for me to remember fairly quickly how to associate the words with the desired actions that they wanted me to perform. I heard somewhere that some human author, Emerson I believe, once said that foolish consistency is the hobgoblin of little minds. I know for a fact that dogs don't have little minds, but consistency in the training regime sure helps in learning things quickly.

Look at it this way. Suppose some aliens from outer space caught you and put you into a room. You were mildly afraid of what they might do. An alien walks into the room. You cower against the wall.

"Ardlarvask!" the alien says, and throws a sweet-smelling piece of German chocolate pie in front of you. You are hungry, so you crouch down, pick up the pie, and stuff it into your mouth.

"Zubilick!" the alien says, and walks out of the room.

The next day, the alien comes back. You are cowering against the wall again.

"Ardlarvask!" the alien says again, and again throws you a piece of German chocolate pie, which you crouch down to get.

As you crouch down, the alien says "Zubilick!" and walks out of the room.

My bet is that it wouldn't take many days for you to begin to realize that when the alien says "Ardlarvask!" you are supposed to crouch down and that you will be getting a piece of pie. Also, my guess is that in a few days you will begin to realize that when the alien says "Zubilick!" you can breathe a sigh of relief, because that means that the alien is about to leave.

Now imagine how long it would take to learn to crouch down if one day the alien said "Ard simpang lar davask," another day the alien said "Da lar simpard vask," another day it was "Simpang ard," and so on.

What nonsense, you say? Then watch someone trying to train their dog sometime.

"Come on, boy, sit!"

"Aw, naw, sit!"

"Pleese, sit now!"

"You can do it, sit, sit, sit, sit, sit!"

So now all of us knew about "Sit," "Down," and "Heel." Con and Judy wanted me to know two more commands, and these were a bit harder to learn. They wanted me to be able to respond to "Stay" and to "Come."

The training regime for "Stay" was relatively simple. Judy would tell me "down," and when I was lying down on the rug, I would get both verbal praise and a food reward. Judy would then say "Stay," and at the same time hold her hand up toward me, like a policeman stopping traffic. I was supposed to lie there until she gave me another command.

Unfortunately, I didn't want to lie there. I wanted to be near Judy, and particularly near those delicious morsels of food. So I would immediately get up and walk over to Judy.

Judy then would say "Naa" in a low-pitched voice, walk me over to the spot where I was lying down, and gently plop me down on the ground, repeating "Stay."

This turned out to be a contest of wills. Since I was not being immediately rewarded with food for staying, I wanted to be out of there and doing something useful, something that would give me food. Judy didn't want to give me any food until I was doing what she wanted me to do, which was to stay in one spot.

Finally, I could see that we were going nowhere with all this, and I decided to stay where I was plopped down.

Judy waited about thirty seconds, to make sure that I wasn't going to move, then said, "Good boy, Zephyr is a good boy!" and there was that magic food!

A few more repetitions of this, and I learned how to do "Stay."

Now we had the last command to learn, the command "Come." This I learned from the "stay" position. Once I was in "Stay," Judy backed off across the living room, got out another morsel of food, and said, "Zephyr, Come!"

I shot across the room, both to be near Judy and to get the food. Judy gave me the food, the verbal praise, and a pat on the head. Oh, heaven!

It took about three weeks for me to learn how to do all of the commands, using the positive reward method. It was simple, fun for all, and painless. I highly recommend it.

Dog Dominance

So why did we have to go through all this business of training? Why couldn't Con and Judy leave me alone to grow up in peace? Well, here we touch on a peculiarity of dog life that is somewhat different from all the peculiarities of human life.

Dogs are hardwired, genetically programmed, to be aware of their status. A dog pack has a dominant male, the alpha male, and a dominant female, the alpha female. The dominant male is usually dominant over the alpha female, and together they are dominant over everyone else in the pack. These are the leaders of the pack, the bosses, and everyone else pays attention to what they say. They solve all the problems, they take care of everything. When they speak up, everyone else has to snap to.

If a subordinate dog doesn't snap to, the dominant gets annoyed. He will go over to the subordinate and put his head on the subordinate's shoulder. This usually causes the subordinate to lie down, turn on his back, and expose his belly. The dominant dog then stands over the subordinate and stares down at the subordinate's eyes. If the dominant dog is really annoyed, he will growl and nip at the subordinate's throat.

In social relationships, dogs are snobs. There is no equality. In a dog pack, you always know exactly where you stand socially with respect to all the other dogs in the pack. Every dog has his or her rank. Although there is only one real dominant, the alpha, some dogs are more dominant than others. In the words of another human writer, all dogs were created equal, but some dogs were created more equal than others. To borrow some words from Con, dogs have a dominance hierarchy – one top dog, one bottom dog, and then a bunch of other dogs, each of which is slightly more dominant than the other.

Equality with a dog doesn't work. If you try to treat your dog as an equal, your dog will be puzzled. Who is in charge here, you or the dog? Who is supposed to be solving problems, who is supposed to be taking care of all the activities of daily life?

But dogs don't stay puzzled for very long. If you show no clear signs of being dominant, your dog decides you are a subordinate, and he or she is the dominant animal in your family pack.

This places a lot of responsibility on her or him. She has to ensure you get up at the right time, observe the proper feeding protocols (she gets fed first), and observe the proper protocols of manners (never annoy the dominant animal). In addition, she has to protect her pack from all outsiders (mailman, boyfriend, girlfriend, stray children). This is a heavy responsibility, and she struggles to cope with the strain of this workload. On top of all that, she quickly notices that her human is getting increasingly more uppity and obnoxious. She tries some simple remedies first, such as putting her head on her human's shoulder or staring at her human, but eventually, she gets annoyed that her human persists in refusing to roll on his back and expose his stomach. She decides that the only rational course of action at this point is to nip the human, to bring him into line. At this point we have a frantic, hysterical human who curses the day he set eyes on that dog of his!

Con and Judy decided that early on I had to be taught that I was not the dominant animal in their household. And the best way to teach me this was to make me go through a series of commands. That way, I had to do what someone else wanted, rather than make someone else do what I wanted. In my mind, as in any dog's mind, if I have to do someone else's bidding, then I am a subordinate, and they are dominant.

From a dog's point of view, there are many advantages to being subordinate. As a subordinate, I do not have to worry about keeping everyone in line. I don't have to worry about defending the house against all comers (although I certainly would defend the house if I sensed that my dominant pack members were in trouble, or if I sensed that someone meant harm to my dominant pack members). I don't have to worry about approving or disapproving of visitors to the house – my dominant pack members are responsible for that chore. I don't have to worry about when I get fed, or about defending my food – I just assume that my dominant pack members will feed me when they feel like it, and if they feel like messing with my food dish, well, they are dominant, so they can do whatever they like.

Being subordinate is a relatively carefree life, compared to the stress of being dominant. The early training I received established in a clear-cut manner that I was subordinate, and Con and Judy continued my training to make sure that I realized that I was still subordinate.

Since I like to think in hierarchies, it is a matter of some interest to me who is more dominant, Con or Judy? Sometimes I think that it is Con, other times I think that it is Judy. Con clearly thinks that he is dominant all the time. Judy, on the other hand, thinks that she is dominant all the time. I wish I could resolve this question. It is very frustrating not to be able to definitively say who the top dog in your pack really is.

Snow Puppy

When I was brought to my new home, Con and Judy talked about how to "toilet train" me. Personally, I thought I was doing just fine – whenever and wherever I needed to go, I went. Unfortunately, neither Con nor Judy seemed to approve of that scenario.

They decided to do several things about this. One was that they would watch me closely, and whenever it looked like I needed to go, they would pick me up and take me outside. Then they would stand near me and say either "pee-pee" or "poop", depending on what they though I was about to do. When I would pee, they would say "pee-pee" over and over again, as well as "good boy!" When I would poop, they would say "poop" many times, as well as the standard "good boy!" According to Con, the whole idea was to get me used to doing what I needed to do in response to these words. Later, I could go on command, assuming I had anything to go with.

Outside, however, was a problem. It was mid-March, the snowiest time of the year where Con and Judy live. Normally, they would have taken me to my dog run, an outside enclosure that was accessible from the house by a set of steep stairs. At this time of year, the enclosure had about two feet of snow in it, and I stood only about ten inches high at the shoulder. Con and Judy were afraid that if they took me out there, I would quickly sink out of sight in the snow, and no one had any St. Bernards around for rescue purposes. On top of this, the stairs were covered with a mixture of snow and ice, and Con was afraid that both he and I would end up in a heap of broken bones if we tried to go down the stairs, either together or separately.

Fortunately, Judy had a solution. An outside covered porch was attached to the bedroom where Con and Judy slept. It got some snow on it whenever the snow was falling, but was covered enough to keep large quantities from piling up, the way the snow did in the dog run. I could be taken out there and encouraged to pee and poop.

It wasn't an ideal solution. Con and Judy talked about it at length, discussing the possibilities. Con felt that it was best to get a dog used to going to the toilet outside as soon as possible. He mentioned that some people like to "paper-train" their puppies to go on newspaper in some convenient place in the house, usually a kitchen or bathroom, and then later when the puppy grows up a little bit, try to switch the ante to going outside. The result is usually a confused puppy that often has difficulty making the switch.

"Sure," Judy said, "I know it's not the best solution. But at this point, what choice do we have? Do you want him to start going in the house?"

"Well," Con said, "since you put it that way, I guess we don't really have any choice. Outside porch it is!"

I caught on fairly quickly. I realized that they didn't want me to go in the house. The trick was in telling them to take me outside, since my bladder was fairly small, and when I would get excited, I wouldn't be able to hold it for very long.

Fortunately, I seemed to be able to communicate with Judy about this right away. I would look at her and think, I have to go!

She would then turn to Con and say, "I think Zephyr needs to go outside. Would you please take him out?"

Con would then turn to me and say, "Zephyr, do you want to go outside?"

I would say, yes! yes! yes! The outward manifestation of that was that I would wag my tail, at which point Con would pick me up and take me outside on the covered porch, where I could wade through the snow until I found a spot that seemed to be just right for whatever I had to do.

Although I found that walking through the snow was cold and mildly unpleasant, it seemed to make a lasting impression on me. Winter was over all too quickly, and I just as quickly forgot about the snow until the following winter. Then, much to everyone's surprise, I found that I loved the snow! I loved running in the snow, I loved walking in the snow, I loved chasing snowballs. Con and Judy were amazed. After all, I was born in California, where the nearest snow was at least one-hundred-fifty miles away. While poodles are well-known for their abilities to swim in water (even our feet are webbed, to allow us to be stronger swimmers), neither Con nor Judy could find out anything about poodles being bred for life in the snow. Finally, Con decided that this was a case of "habitat imprinting."

As Con explains it, imprinting is a rapid form of learning, usually at a very young age, that allows animals to learn who their parents are. In dogs, this period of rapid learning takes place between the ages of approximately five weeks and twelve weeks for a puppy. At this time, the puppy learns through the process of imprinting to be affectionate to whoever interacts with him or her. At five weeks, it is usually the puppy's mom and its litter mates. When a puppy is bought at the age of eight weeks (as I happened to be when I found Con and Judy), the puppy has already been exposed to dogs and is now ready to be exposed to people. This is the optimum time because there are still about four weeks left of the imprinting period during which the puppy can learn who its people are. Much beyond twelve weeks, and a dog has a much more difficult time learning to be affectionate to people. And if people buy a puppy much before it is eight weeks old, the dog never really learns how to socialize very well with other dogs. So this time is very critical to a dog's happy life.

Con thought that in addition to imprinting on humans, I also imprinted on snow. He said that some studies have suggested that birds imprint on the habitats where they grew up, returning to those habitats after migrating to southern latitudes for the winter. Then, being carried away in a total flight of fancy, he started speculating that maybe even people imprint on the habitat where they grew up, so that people who grew up around snow like to live in (or at least visit) snow country, while people who grew up where it doesn't snow never feel really comfortable when the white flakes start piling up on the ground.

But I digress. All this toilet training was fine as long as Con and Judy were around to watch me all the time. However, there were times during the day when they both had to be gone, and at night they both valued their sleep. So they decided to get a box.

The box was a standard airline-type dog crate made of plastic, with a metal door that could be latched. The idea was, according to Con, that it would give me a safe place to be, where I could feel secure, as if I was in a cave or in a burrow like the kind used by my doggish ancestors way back when. An added benefit, again according to Con, was that during the night, or whenever both Con and Judy had to be gone, I could be locked into the box. There I would be safe from the perils of chewing on furniture. There I would also be safe from the perils of peeing on the rug, because dogs hate to pee or poop in the same immediate place where they have to sleep.

I was to be confined to the box during the night, and whenever Con and Judy weren't home. I was also to be confined to the box for several hours each afternoon, regardless of whether or not anyone was home, on the theory that I needed to get plenty of rest.

The first night in the box, Con and Judy set up the crate in their bedroom, near their bed. They put in a comfortable mat and also put in about five towels so that I would have something to snuggle up against and so that I would stay warm.

Then they put me in the box, gave me lots of reassuring words, and turned off the lights.

I was worried.

I wanted to be with them, in or at least on their bed, snuggled up to Judy. I certainly didn't want to be inside a plastic crate. Yes, I could smell both Con and Judy. Yes, I could hear both Con and Judy. But, I couldn't feel them, I couldn't touch them, I couldn't lick them.

I felt alone and abandoned. I started to cry.

"Con, I don't think Zephyr likes his box," said Judy.

"He has to get used to it," said Con.

Whine, yelp, whine, yelp, yelp, said Zephyr.

After a few minutes, Judy said, "We have to do something!"

She got up, rummaged around in the closet, and came up with an old sweatshirt. This she put outside the door of the crate.

I stuck my nose into the metal bars of the door of the crate. I could feel Judy! I could smell Judy! I could lick Judy! With that, I fell asleep, much to everyone's relief.

The box stayed with me for about a year. I guess it worked as a toilet training tool because I never did anything inside the crate. Even if I really had to go and Con and Judy were gone for a few hours, I would hold it in until they came home. Then I would yelp and be let out immediately into the outside dog run.

As a place of safety, a secure and warm place where I could go when I was tired, the box was a miserable failure. I hated being inside the box when Con and Judy were home and I was supposed to be resting. I always felt that I could rest much better in their lap, or at their feet, than I could rest inside my crate. Sure, I could sleep inside the box without any distractions. But that's not what life is all about. Life is about being with those you love, and that means sitting in their lap.

When I got older, about a year old, Con suggested to Judy that they consider letting me stay in the house, outside the box, whenever they were both gone. Judy greeted that suggestion with caution. She was afraid that I would chew on the furniture, or get into something that I wasn't supposed to and hurt myself. Little did she realize that I was willing to be on my best behavior, just to stay out of the box.

Con persisted, and finally Judy agreed to try leaving me out. They went away for about an hour. Oh, heaven! I didn't have to go into the box! At first, I was a little scared. What if someone broke in? What was I supposed to do? Bark, yes, but what else? When I was in the box, if someone broke into the house, it wasn't my problem – there was nothing I could do about it, shut up into a crate. But now, it was a different story.

Seri taunted me. Here you were, trying to get them to keep you out of the box for months, and now you're scared? You, a big dog? If someone breaks in, I'll tell you what to do, said Seri.

'This didn't particularly reassure me, since Seri's version of what to do whenever a stranger came into the house was to run and hide under the bed. Unfortunately, I was too big to hide under the bed. Besides, my dog genes wouldn't have let me do that, anyway.

As the minutes ticked by and no one broke into the house, I became more and more confident. It was wonderful to be able to run around, sniff everything, explore everything, without a human hanging over your shoulder. I felt very pleased with myself. Now I was really a big dog, guardian and protector of the house.

Nevertheless, I was pretty happy to see Con and Judy come home after an hour. Responsibility for the welfare of the house is a weighty matter, and I was glad to turn it over to the humans when they walked in the door.

Now I stay home alone as a matter of course, guarding and protecting the house. I am always happy to see Con and Judy come home because that means that I can socialize with them, but I am no longer worried about my ability to chase away any intruders. I always have the run of the house, and sleep on a mat at the foot of Con and Judy's bed. That way, I can run downstairs and investigate if there is any suspicious noise. However, to tell the truth, I value my sleep most nights, and since Con and Judy are dominant to me in the household hierarchy, I am willing to let them deal with suspicious noises. Only if they call for my help will I wake up at night.

The time came when the box was finally dismantled and taken down to the garage. I was both happy and sad to see it go. Happy because I never really liked it. Sad because it was my puppyhood, slipping away from me, never to return.

HOME ALONE

A couple of months after they brought me home, Con and Judy decided that they needed to go shopping for a variety of things that were unavailable in the small town where we lived. That meant an all-day expedition to the city. The question was, what to do with me? I would have liked to have gone along, and I politely kept requesting that they consider that possibility. In fact, they did consider that option and promptly rejected it because in summer, a car heats up a lot when it is standing in the sun.

I did not understand. I thought that I could go wherever they went, without any problems. Since then, I have talked to other dogs whose humans have taken them out shopping in the middle of the summer. Most of the dogs I've talked to don't recommend the experience. Imagine this – you are all eager to go and see the world. You are happy to be going out with your humans. Suddenly, they park the car somewhere in the hot sun, open up the windows a crack, and vanish! At first, you are still excited. Then you notice that it is getting rather warm. Warmer, warmer, the car is getting warmer. You could fry eggs on the dashboard if you were a short-order cook. You get very thirsty and would like something to drink, but there is no water. Soon, you are extremely hot, and there is no way to get out of the heat. What to do? I have known dogs who have peed all over themselves to try to cool themselves down. And then, just when you think you are about to die of heat stroke, your people come back and get mad at YOU for messing up the car seats. Not a pretty picture.

Con and Judy talked about putting me into the box, but decided against that, since I would have to be there for about ten hours.

"Let's put Zephyr into the dog run in the backyard," said Con.

"Do you think he'll be all right there?" asked Judy.

"Sure. The day is warm, there is lots of shade, and he can look at the neighbors. That should keep him happy and amused."

"Yes, and he can use the fresh air, and sleep in the sun."

So I was bundled off to the backyard. To make sure that I would have a secure place to go if I got scared, I had an igloo-type dog house that I could go into. To ensure that no one could enter the dog run and steal me, the gate to the run had a sturdy lock.

Con and Judy left, convinced I would amuse myself by watching the birds, the bees, and perhaps the neighbors.

The trouble was, the birds and the bees were amusing for about five minutes. The neighbors were entertaining for another ten minutes. Fifteen minutes down, and nine and a half hours to go!

After about an hour, I started to get lonely and started to cry.

I am sometimes amazed at what humans don't know about dogs. Dogs are social creatures. We evolved a social system that calls for life in a pack. That means that most of the time, ancestral dogs, way back when, were with other dogs. They slept together, ate together, hunted together, and socialized together. If a dog got separated from the pack, he would howl and bark, and bark and howl, until other pack members would start to bark and howl in return. That would allow the lost dog to find the pack, and rejoin the social group. A dog separated from his pack is an anxious dog.

Now humans come along and decide that a dog is going to have fun sitting in a yard by himself. They can't seem to understand why a dog starts to bark and howl under these circumstances.

"John, it's getting dark. Time to put the dog outside in the back yard, so she can sleep in her doghouse," says a human who doesn't understand us.

"Sure, Jane. The dog will enjoy the smells and sounds of the night. Besides, we don't want her underfoot," says the other human. Out goes the dog.

Soon the dog starts to bark and howl.

"John, can't you make the dog shut up?"

"Sure, Jane," says John. He walks to the door, opens it, screams, "Shadduppp!" and slams the door in the face of the poor dog, who thought that at last she was going to be let inside to rejoin her pack.

The dog barks and howls even more loudly.

"John, wassamater with the dog? She nuts or something?"

"I dunno, Jane. Let's ignore her. She's gonna get tired of barking, or wear out her vocal cords eventually."

Night turns into day, and the dog is still barking and howling. The neighbors are worn out from trying to sleep and failing miserably. John and Jane can't figure out why their dog is barking, and decide that they have a stupid, psycho dog. Eventually, they tune out the barking completely and don't even hear it. Usually, the neighbors aren't that lucky.

The solution is simple. Let the dog inside! When the dog rejoins her pack, she is happy and stops barking, and pretty soon, the neighbors are happy, too.

So there I was, barking, whimpering, and howling. The neighbor kids came by and talked to me occasionally, which somewhat cheered me up. Still, it was a long ten hours, particularly when it started to get dark.

In case you don't know it, dogs can't see very well in the dark. In fact, even under the best circumstances, our vision isn't as good as an average human's, much as I hate to admit it. We see colors (the idea that dogs are colorblind is a fantasy). We see shapes. But we can't see the kinds of details that humans can see. And this gets worse when it gets dark. Then we have to rely primarily on our nose and our ears.

Curiously enough, even dog relatives such as wolves and coyotes apparently see better in the daytime than they do at night. So why do they hunt at night? Con says that there are several theories. One theory suggests that it is harder for prey to escape from a wolf pack or from a coyote at night when neither the predators nor the prey can see all that well. Another theory suggests that both wolves and coyotes used to hunt in the daytime, and then people came along and shot the wolves and coyotes. In self-defense, the wolves and coyotes started to hunt at night, when people couldn't see all that well to shoot.

For a four-month-old puppy, the noises and smells of the night are particularly frightening. Especially when you're all alone, abandoned by your pack. Skunks snuffle by outside your pen, filling up your nose with an acrid stench that momentarily makes you incapable of smelling anything else (if you think that this is trivial, imagine something going past your house at night that makes you totally blind for about ten minutes – now, is that scary, or what?). Deer rustle in the bushes. Bats swoop down with a series of high-pitched squeaks that make your ears ring with pain. Who knows what these animals could do to a poor, lonely puppy?

Finally, finally, Con and Judy came home and let me into the house. I thought about sulking and not greeting them to show my displeasure at their thoughtless behavior of leaving me outside. But I was simply too glad to see them, and too happy to be back with my pack. Even Seri the cat looked good just then!

That summer, Con and Judy left me alone in the backyard on several occasions. Each time I was miserable. Then came the blessed time when Con and Judy were willing to leave me alone in the house while they went off for several hours.

Now you might think that being inside the house, practically alone, is just as bad as being outside in the yard. However, it's not the same, at all. Inside the house, I have my familiar places, my familiar smells. I have my bed. I have a couch to crawl up on. I can go blissfully to sleep and not have a care in the world, except for wondering when Con and Judy will be home.

WALK THE DOG

When I was about four months old, I got my last parvo shot, and Con and Judy decided that it was all right to take me outside for walks. They didn't want to take me outside before that time, because parvo is a terrible disease, particularly for puppies, and the virus that causes parvo can live for up to a year wherever sick dogs have been. It can be a serious problem sometimes, particularly because some dog owners refuse or neglect to immunize their dogs. Some people believe that dogs should live a "natural life", and that life apparently does not include immunizations. Most dogs that live a "natural life" usually live a short life, and die in horrible agony.

So, I was trundled off in the car to some nearby woods for a walk.

Oh, joy! I cannot describe to you what a walk in the woods feels like to a dog. Our sense of smell is about a million times more sensitive than the human sense of smell. Our hearing is much more acute. We can hear frequencies well in the ultrasonic range, well outside the range of human hearing. We can smell a deer that has passed by a tree four days ago. We can hear a gopher burrowing two feet underground.

Off I went, running around in all directions, smelling everything, listening to everything.

Most humans think that dogs like walks because of the exercise. Sure, that's part of it, but it's only a small part. The main part of a walk is the intellectual exercise. We like daily walks the same way humans like watching the news on TV or reading the newspaper. Sort of a news of the day, catch up on what's going on. When we run around in familiar places, we can catch up on what other dogs have been there, what other animals have come by, what plants have started to bloom, and lots of other things that are relevant to a dog's life. When we walk around in unfamiliar places, we can explore new smells, try to identify new animals and plants and stretch our brains a little. A walk for a dog is like the sports page, the gossip columns, and the comics, all wrapped up into a fun-filled time.

I suppose I'm lucky, living in an area with woods and wilderness areas. There is always some new place that I can explore. Con and Judy like to go to new places, and quickly get bored with going to the same place over and over again. For me, going to the same place is never boring. Why is that, you might ask? Because for me, just like for any dog, the same place is never the same place. It always changes. New things are always happening. A cat walks by at midnight. At ten the next morning, we can smell that cat. A skunk changes its foraging route. We pick that up right away. Sameness is just something that humans, handicapped by their duller senses, believe in because they don't know any better. The reality is that the world is a constantly changing place, regardless of where you are.

So for me, there are always new places where I can stretch my brain. But if I lived in the city and had to go for walks around the same city blocks, day after day, it would be no tragedy. Things in the city change just as much as things in the country. Cities have dogs and cats who roam, leaving odor trails behind. Cities have rats, cockroaches, pigeons, sparrows, grasshoppers, and many other interesting creatures that can be looked at, smelled, and heard. Cities have grass and flowers. Cities have trees and leaves. Nothing is ever the same, from one day to the next. Each day brings new challenges, intellectual stimulation, and for many dogs, a time when they snap out of the boredom of their lives.

Think about it. What does your average dog do all day? Sleep. Eat. Sleep. The average dog interacts with its humans for a part of the day, but most humans work, go to school, go shopping, go out to eat, or do other activities that make them unavailable for interacting with the family dog. What is the result? Sheer boredom! What can the dog do about it? Sleep! And wait eagerly for the times when he or she can go for a walk.

Being taken for walks raised a difference of opinion between Con and Judy. Con felt that I should always be on a leash, for my protection and safety. Judy felt that I should be allowed to run free, both as a way of exercising my muscles and as a way of letting me explore my surroundings. The result of this difference of opinion was that when Con would take me for a walk, he would keep me on an expandable leash. When Judy would take me for a walk, she would let me run free.

Let me just say that in cities, you should never let a dog off a leash. There are too many possibilities for the dog to get hurt. Something can startle a dog, causing it to run out into traffic. Or, the dog can tangle with an unfriendly dog, to the detriment of both dogs and owners.

In the woods, however, it's a different story. Con's perspective is that there are lots of things that can go wrong in the woods, just like in a city. I could start chasing a deer, lose my bearings, and wind up getting lost. I could find something inappropriate to eat and get sick. I could run off and get attacked by a mountain lion or a bear.

I disagree very strongly with Con's perspective. I have tried to get across the idea that I will be on my best behavior when out in the woods. Sure, I will chase deer, and birds, and squirrels. But, I won't get lost, and I'll always come back. After all, if I get lost, who will take care of my people? A lot of times I think that they can't cross the street unassisted, much less do without me for everything else they do in their life. I think that where it's reasonably safe, a dog should be allowed to run. Yes, there are risks, but where aren't there risks in life?

I have tried to get my point across to Con. The result has been that sometimes he lets me run free, and other times he keeps me on an expandable leash. This disgusts me, and I'm keeping on working on him to have a more balanced perspective.

While we are on the subject of leashes, let me comment a bit on leash etiquette. I've seen a lot of dogs taken for walks on leashes, and most times the humans haven't known what to do to make the walk enjoyable for everyone. Dogs like to smell, and we get excited about our outings. As a result, we pull on our leashes, wanting to get to all the interesting smells just out of our reach. The typical dog-walking person then pulls back on the leash, so that we have a constriction around our throat and chest. The typical dog responds to any constriction around the throat or chest by pulling, to free itself. Now we have dog pulling human, and human pulling dog, which doesn't make anyone happy.

The solution is simple. Whenever possible, get an expandable leash, and let your dog run around smelling things. If the dog persists in pulling, as some of our more excitable members of the species are occasionally known to do, give a brief, sharp tug, accompanied by some word of displeasure such as "Naah!" The tug has to be brief, otherwise the dog's genetic programming against constrictions will kick in, and the dog will pull even harder. Just enough of a tug is necessary to get the dog's attention.

Where an expandable leash is not possible, teach your dog to heel. I can't believe how many people have trouble with this. It's a relatively simple process. You have the leash on a harness, and you're ready to go. But, you say, my dog runs off right away, pulling me behind. Wrong! You start out, and if your dog starts to pull on the leash, give the leash a tug, say "heel!", turn around and walk in the opposite direction. Your dog is faced with a choice: turn around and follow you, or be pulled backwards. No dog likes to be pulled backwards, so we turn around and follow. If we run ahead, do it again. And again. And again. The object is to get the dog to walk beside you, with the leash hanging loose in your hand. Not tight. Not choking. Loose. Some of us might not be geniuses at this (either dogs or owners, I will concede here), so it may take a lot of repetition. But remember, be consistent! Do it the same every time, and do it often! Relatively quickly, you will have a dog who will trot along at your side without pulling.

And if your dog can't or won't learn how to walk next to you without pulling, there is the Gentle Leader. This is a harness designed by some animal behaviorists that keeps almost all dogs from pulling. It fits over the nose and the back of the neck, and the leash attaches to the bottom of the harness, under the nose. If a dog pulls, the nose comes down, and immediately the dog is no longer interested in pulling. In a very gentle way, anyone can get control over their dog.

Now comes your part of the bargain. Once your dog is willing to walk alongside you, let your dog stop and smell the roses. Don't be in such a hurry that every time your dog wants to stop and sniff, you give a yank and off you go. Believe me, this is not fun for your dog. And, if it's not fun for your dog, your dog will have no incentive to cooperate with you on having a good time during a walk. Relax, and you'll both have a good time.

Another part of leash etiquette involves meeting strange dogs who are on leashes of their own. This is a tricky problem, and if you do it wrong, you could teach your dog to be suspicious of other dogs.

Let me use Con as an example. Con is always afraid that when I get near another dog, he or she will attack me. Why he is afraid, I don't know. I am a big dog, and most of the dogs I meet would have a hard time opening up their mouths wide enough just to bite me. But there it is – he is still afraid that I'm going to get bitten.

As we approach another dog, Con pulls on my leash to hold me back. Me, I'm just happy to meet another dog. As a poodle, I'm a persistent optimist. Every new dog represents a happy adventure.

I wag my tail, the other dog wags his tail. But Con pulls on the leash.

"Is your dog friendly?" Con asks the other dog owner.

Now, this is a stupid question. No one is going to reply: "No, my dog eats poodles for breakfast, and polishes off several cats for dessert!"

The answer is always, "Oh, yes, my dog loves other dogs!"

This answer is given regardless of whether their dog is wagging his tail, or has raised his hackles, bared his teeth, and is growling loudly.

So, Con keeps pulling on my leash, thinking "Oh, my God! That dog could bite Zephyr!"

The other dog owner, meanwhile, is also pulling on his dog's leash, thinking "Oh, my God! That enormous dog could gulp down my dog in one swallow!"

Both owners are now transmitting their nervousness to their dogs.

The dogs pick up on this and think, if my person is so nervous, maybe something here calls for a fear response or an aggressive re-sponse. Maybe I should defend my person against this other dog. This dog seems to be friendly, but since my human is so afraid of her, maybe I should bite her to cause her to go away.

The end result is that the dog is conditioned to respond with fear or aggression when meeting other dogs.

The right way to do it is to be perfectly unconcerned. Let your dog stroll over to the other dog, and let them both go through all the proper dog protocols. Dogs have anal glands near the base of their tails, and they like to sniff those glands on other dogs. Then they like to sniff each other's muzzles. Give your dog a loose leash, so that he or she can have enough room to go through all the doggish greetings. As long as both owners are relaxed about the whole thing, everything will usually be fine. If the dogs start acting up and growling or snarling, then one or both owners can get their dog out of there quickly.

I'm still working on Con to relax about other dogs. He's better now than he was before, but he still gets nervous in the endearingly mulish way that people have of holding on to their cherished habits. He should know better.

Bad Dogs

Before you get the idea that all dogs are good, let me tell you that it isn't so. There are some bad dogs out there. Some of these dogs are the product of bad genetics. Others have been made that way by people.

As a poodle, I always have an optimistic view of everything. That includes dog behavior – I always think that every dog I meet will be a nice, friendly, well-behaved dog. But after being bitten by another dog, I have learned to be a little wary, even though I still hope for the best.

We were out in the woods, Con and I, and I was running around without a leash. I was having a great time. Suddenly, over the crest of a hill appeared a Rottweiler.

Con immediately got worried and yelled, "Zephyr, come!"

I heard Con, but I thought it would be much more interesting to play with another dog than to obey the command. I decided I would come over and say hello to the Rottweiler, so I ran up and prepared myself for the usual dog protocols. Instead, the dog lunged forward and sank his teeth into my back.

I couldn't believe it. I hadn't done anything to provoke the attack. I was just being me.

I yelped, got free, and ran off. Con was yelling and running toward me, but he was still some distance away. I thought, there must be some mistake here. Maybe the Rottweiler thought that I was a deer or a piece of meat. Maybe he's nearsighted. Maybe he can't smell that I'm a dog. Let's go up to him again, and introduce myself. Surely, once he realizes that I'm a friendly dog, he'll want to make friends and run around and play.

Up I went to the dog, and chomp went his teeth into my side. I yelped again and ran off.

Con finally arrived and started yelling at the dog. Con was furious. Even though I knew he liked dogs, I was afraid that he would try to throttle that particular dog. Since he had his solid oak hiking stick with him, that seemed like it was a real possibility.

The Rottweiler appraised the situation. A friendly poodle he could handle, hands down. A now not-so-friendly poodle and an angry human was a somewhat different proposition. He decided that discretion was the better part of valor, and took off at a casual pace over the crest of the nearest hill.

Con immediately took me home and cleaned up my bites. Fortunately, my fur was long, cushioning the impact of the teeth, so the bites weren't very deep. The worst part was having to endure a lecture from Con:

"Zephyr, a dog like that could have killed you! You have to be a little smarter. Don't always assume that every dog you meet is going to be your friend. And, you stupid dog, when I call you, you come immediately. Is that understood?"

While I resented being called a stupid dog, I had to admit that in this one case, Con seemed to know what he was talking about. I hung my head and mildly wagged my tail, letting Con know I was sorry, at least for the next ten minutes.

Later, Con found out that the Rottweiler was owned by some people who thought the dog should protect them from robbers and muggers. This meant, in their mind (and I'm not convinced that they had much mind), that they had to have a mean dog. So they abused the poor animal. They would yell at the dog, hit the dog, chain up the dog in their yard, and were generally nasty. Naturally, the dog didn't like anyone. The poor dog probably didn't much like himself either. Even for a Rottweiler, it's really tough on your self-esteem when everyone treats you like dirt. Eventually, you just feel like lashing out. Too bad it was me at the end of the dog's teeth, rather than his owner's leg. The owners deserved to be bitten – I didn't.

Con says that genetics also can contribute to bad dog behavior. Some dogs are raised in puppy mills by unscrupulous breeders who are only interested in turning a fast buck. These people can inbreed dogs like crazy to get the maximum number of puppies. If you've forgotten what inbreeding is, it is when you mate close relatives together. Brother-sister, father-daughter, mother-son, that kind of thing. Humans usually have taboos about it as far as they themselves are concerned, for a very good reason – inbreeding does bad things to people. When you inbreed dogs to close genetic relatives, you can have all sorts of genetic defects expressed that would never have shown up if you mated your dog with a genetic stranger. It's not a pretty picture: twisted legs, misshaped heads. These are easy for breeders to spot, and they "cull" these dogs (a euphemism for kill – humans seem to like euphemisms, like putting a dog "to sleep," while we dogs prefer to tell it like it is). Anatomical deformities are easy to eliminate from the gene pool, but behavioral deformities are a lot harder to detect, particularly when your sole interest is to move the puppy out of the breeding area so that you can raise more puppies. You can get really fearful dogs, you can get really aggressive dogs, and worst of all, you can get the psycho dogs that seem fine most of the time, then turn on everyone and bite. A lot of little kids are bitten this way by the family dog who was loving and kind a few minutes before turning nasty.

I just heard the other day about a golden retriever that bit a little kid. Unbelievable! All the golden retrievers that I know are nice, mellow, family dogs. They like to chew a lot, particularly as puppies, but chewing on friends and family, never! Puppy mills have done it again!

Yes, there are bad dogs out there. But, most of these bad dogs have been created by people through intentional abuse or faulty breeding practices. Either way, someone suffers, and it's usually not the abuser or the puppy mill breeder.

Good Food, Bad Food

One problem with letting dogs run free, I admit, is that we are suckers for picking up morsels of food from the ground. The food can be perfectly good, or it can be spoiled, in which case we can get sick. We just can't seem to resist – when something smells delicious, our genes kick in, and we scarf it down as quickly as possible.

From the human standpoint, what smells good to us can be disgusting to our humans. My particular weakness is poop. I love eating it. Con and Judy are disgusted by it.

As a connoisseur, I can tell you that there's poop and there's great poop. Ordinary poop is what your run-of-the-mill carnivore leaves, like a cat or dog. It can be nutritious, but it has a kind of recycled flavor. I generally avoid that kind.

Great poop is the kind that comes from herbivores, like rabbits, deer, antelope, and elk. It is loaded with fibrous plant material and gut bacteria – the combination tastes wonderful. I try to eat it whenever I can, although my opportunities are greatly limited by Con and Judy, who try to keep me from eating any of it.

I know enough about people to know what you are thinking – this is a horrible dog with a terrible habit.

Let me set you straight. Poop-eating is something that all mammals do, to some extent. Even humans have been known to do it. Anthropologists call it by the fancy name of coprophagy, which in plain English means "poop eating." For all mammals, it is probably an important source of gut bacteria and information about what the other guy dined on the night before. Among the herbivores, babies often eat their parents' poop to get the bacteria and enzymes that they need to handle plant foods. The carnivores probably get a variety of vitamins, trace elements, and unused proteins out of poop. So, all around, it is an important source of nutrients and information.

Now, your typical dog owner – like Con and Judy – is going to try to keep a dog from eating poop. If the dog persists, a visit to the vet might ensue.

The vet will say something like, "Perhaps the food that you are feeding him is not nutritious enough. Try Brand X, which I happen to have on hand, and see if that helps." Let me tell you, it won't.

Or, perhaps, the vet will say, "Maybe your dog is simply bored, and has nothing better to do than to eat poop. Try cleaning up immediately after him, and don't let him get close to other dogs' poop. See if that helps." Again, it won't.

Poop-eating is a normal part of being a dog. You can take the poop away from a dog, but you can't take away the taste for poop. Even if it makes us sick, we love eating it when and where possible.

We also love to eat anything else that might taste good. One day, that habit got me into some serious trouble.

Judy and I were taking a walk on some Forest Service land that was leased to a rancher. I was having a great time running around, off my leash, when I suddenly ran across a piece of meat that had been dead for a while. It sort of smelled funny, but what the hey, food is food, so I grabbed it and held it in my mouth.

Judy saw that I had something, and yelled, "Zephyr, drop that right now! Drop!"

Well, if Judy didn't want me to eat it, and it was food, it probably was something really good. Maybe it was something she wanted to eat herself, like the delicious things that Con and Judy eat at dinner, and yell at me for trying to steal morsels from the table.

I quickly swallowed it, before Judy could catch me. All told, I felt quite pleased with myself.

Unfortunately, I swallowed poisoned meat that had been scattered around to kill coyotes. Soon, I got really sick.

But let me digress for a moment. Part of growing up involves finding out about the stupidity of your elders. In my case, growing up involves finding out about the stupidity of some humans. Coyotes are part of the natural ecology of the land. As a carnivore (really an omnivore, since coyotes eat just about anything), they eat a variety of small animals, such as rabbits, lizards, snakes, small birds, and various insects. They prevent these other animal species from building up to such large population sizes that they strip the land of all the available food and then starve to death. They are part of the balance of nature. Mostly, they hunt alone, but occasionally, they will hunt in pairs, and very rarely, they will hunt in a pack. When they hunt alone, they catch mostly small animals. When they hunt in a pack, they can kill larger animals, such as deer and elk.

Sure, occasionally coyotes might kill young cows or young sheep. Is that sufficient reason to poison them, or shoot them on sight? Snow storms, rock slides, floods, and rain will occasionally kill cows and sheep. That, too, is part of the balance of nature. On the whole, coyotes do much more good for us than they do harm. Yet humans

mindlessly poison and shoot them. Poisoning is particularly bad because the poison travels up the food chain. A poisoned animal is eaten
by vultures, ravens, hawks, and eagles, who all become poisoned and
die. If the poison is particularly nasty, it kills anything that then, in
turn, eats those vultures, ravens, hawks, and eagles.

One poisoned coyote spells a local ecological disaster. Yet some
ranchers, occasional hunters, and a few state and federal agents persist
in trying to wipe out the coyotes, just as they waged a fierce and
successful fight against wolves in the past.

And I became a victim of this battle. Very soon my stomach started
to cramp, and waves of pain shot through my abdomen. I couldn't
hold anything inside me, everything was coming out at both ends. I
thought I was going to die.

Con and Judy realized that I was probably poisoned, and immediately took me to the vet. The vet gave me some stuff to coat my
stomach and slow down the absorption of the poison.

Fortunately, I ate a very small piece of poisoned meat, and probably
there was a very small quantity of poison that made it into my digestive
system. Prompt veterinary treatment saved my life. Despite all that,
I was very sick for about a week. I couldn't keep anything down, my
gut was a constant stream of diarrhea, and I generally felt miserable.
Con and Judy tried to get me to eat by boiling lean hamburger meat
and offering little pieces to me. I wanted to eat, but every time I
swallowed a little piece, I would throw up and have diarrhea. My
stomach cramped all the time, and just when I thought that it couldn't
hurt any worse than it was already hurting, it would start hurting even
worse than that.

Gradually, I recovered. It was still hard for me to eat anything other
than boiled meat for about a month, as my stomach lining repaired

itself. Eventually, I got back to eating pretty much anything, although even now, my stomach gets upset more easily than it should.

Mind you, I am a peaceful dog, and I don't wish any ill will toward anyone. But, I must admit, I occasionally have dreams about that time. In those dreams, I find the rancher or government agent who was responsible for spreading that poison. I take that person to a room, lock him in, and feed him all the things that make people sick. I see him there, with the worst case of turista that you can imagine.

And then, when he is at his lowest point, I ask him:

"So, how does it feel? This is what it feels like for a coyote or another animal that has eaten your poison. Do you like it? What is your perspective now that YOU are on the receiving end? Are you having fun yet?"

I see him there, scared and miserable, just as I was scared and miserable, just as lots of coyotes are scared and miserable as they die a lonely death.

But then the dream turns into a nightmare. This person, retching his guts out, still does not understand. He still cannot empathize with his fellow creatures, he still cannot see what havoc he is causing. Perhaps he cannot understand. Perhaps he is incapable of understanding. Perhaps he is so caught up with his narrow view of the world that his mind rejects completely any larger picture.

My nightmare ends with a terrible vision. In it, I see all the mammals and birds gone, victims of mindless extermination, and habitats lost to parking lots. I see the forests and the plants gone. Because of the increased demands for space from a rapidly increasing human population and a general lack of food, all the dogs and cats are gone. Nothing else remains but people jammed into little warrens, competing for food with cockroaches. But cockroaches are much more adaptable than humans, and soon nothing else remains but cockroaches.

And then I wake up, feeling sad for the future of the human race. Yes, people are beginning to appreciate the balance of nature, and some ranchers, some hunters, and some government agents are beginning to appreciate the role of coyotes and other predators in controlling the population sizes of other animal species. But many still have a long way to go. Yes, people are getting a more enlightened understanding of ecology and nature, but is it soon enough?

WASH THE DOG

E very evening before I went to bed, I would go out to pee. I would go down the stairs into my run, find a place that looks and smells right, and proceed to mark my territory.

One evening, much to my surprise, I found a skunk in my run. The skunk was surprised too, and a minute later so were Con and Judy. On such an innocent note began the "wash-the-dog" saga.

Let me back up a minute. Normally, skunks don't come into my run. The smell of my pee is probably enough to keep them away. However, a few days before the skunk appeared, Judy put a bird feeder on a branch of the tree in my run. She filled the feeder with sunflower seeds and the birds flocked to the food. Yes, there still is an occasional free lunch here and there in the world. But birds are messy eaters. For every sunflower seed that they eat, they seem to drop ten or twenty onto the ground, leaving the floor of my run covered with little black bundles of food.

Skunks usually like to eat insects, but bugs are sometimes hard to come by on a cool evening. And if you can't find bugs and you're a hungry skunk, why not forage on sunflower seeds?

So, an adventurous skunk decided to do just that. First, he had to fit his pudgy body through the gap between the gate and the fence of my run. This he did with some difficulty, but once he was inside, bonanza! Enough food to put on a pound or so for winter.

He was eating happily when Con opened the door for me, and I ran into my run. I wasn't expecting anything to be there and ran right past the skunk, who was eating next to the stairs that I used to get to where I wanted to pee. In fact, I was so intent on peeing that I stepped right over the skunk before I realized that there was someone else there. The skunk was so intent on eating that he didn't notice me until I was well past him.

Con saw the skunk and immediately called out,

"Zephyr, come!"

Well, the master calls, and I tried to obey. The problem was that to come to Con I had to step over the skunk again, to get to the stairs going up to the house.

The skunk wanted no part of this. Up went his tail, and he turned toward me.

I didn't know anything about skunks, so I took a step toward the stairs.

Suddenly, a blast of warm acrid liquid hit my face and my chest. I immediately wanted to sneeze and wanted to rub my face in the dirt. I took a few steps backward, unsure about what to do.

Con wanted me out of there, so he yelled, "Come!" again. Stupid thing to do. Once again, I tried to come, and once again, I got blasted with skunk spray.

So there we were, at a standoff. The skunk was standing at the base of the stairs, tail up and hind end toward me. I was standing about six feet away, not about to try to run toward the skunk again.

Fortunately for everyone, Con and Judy's friend Jim was walking past the dog run. With quick presence of mind, he opened the gate, grabbed my collar, and hauled me out of the run. He took me around to the front door and deposited me into Judy's arms. Meanwhile, the skunk decided that free lunches notwithstanding, dog runs are not healthy places. He squeezed past the gate and hightailed it for parts unknown.

Needless to say, Judy was upset and horrified. Have you ever smelled fresh skunk secretions, really close up? If you haven't, you've missed out on one of the finer things life offers. Perhaps you've smelled a dead skunk on the road. The smell is something like tar, with kind of a musky odor thrown in for good measure. Well, let me tell you, fresh skunk secretion is nothing like the roadkill version. Fresh skunk smells like acrid burning rubber, only one hundred times as strong. You feel like retching, and so does anyone else within about ten feet of you.

"Con, what do we do now?" said Judy.

"I guess we wash the dog," said Con.

"Do you realize that it's ten o'clock at night, and we have to get up early tomorrow?" said Judy.

"Well, what choice do we have?" asked Con.

Complicating the picture somewhat was Jim. Having gallantly retrieved me by the collar, he had smeared some of the skunk secretions onto his arm, which now stank like a tire dump that was being burned illegally. This was bad enough, but on top of that, he had just been on his way to pick up his girlfriend after her job, and he was already running late. Obviously, he couldn't drive anywhere until something was done about his arm.

"Do we have any tomato juice?" asked Con.

"No, but we have about eight cans of tomato paste," said Judy. "Con, hold onto Zephyr while I go open up the cans and see if I can mix some water into the paste."

I've been told by some other dogs that tomato juice for skunks spray is an old wives tale. Each of these dogs has his or her own recipe for what works: vinegar, warm water and shampoo, orange juice. None of these dogs has been sprayed by a skunk, however. All the ones I've talked to who have had the honor of experiencing a skunk's hind end invariably swear by tomato juice.

In any case, Con and Judy were desperate and didn't know about any remedy other than tomatoes.

"Jim, come on into the bathroom and we'll do your arm first," said Judy.

She splashed some of the tomato paste and water concoction on Jim's arm, reducing the smell from retchingly outrageous to merely offensive. Jim felt that he had to hurry, so he rushed out the door.

Now came my turn. I wasn't pleased with the smell, so I squirmed all over the place, smearing the secretions onto Con's arms.

"Where can we wash Zephyr?" asked Con.

"I guess the only place we can do it is in the shower," said Judy.

I was hauled into the bathroom. The shower is a combination shower-bathtub, with glass doors that keep the water from spilling out onto the floor.

Con lifted me into the tub, while Judy took off her clothes and, trying to breathe as little as possible, climbed into the tub with me.

Both Con and Judy smeared my face and chest with the tomato paste, and then Judy washed it off with the shower water. This reduced the smell by a small fraction, but I still stank to high heaven.

"We have to do it again," said Judy.

"We've used up most of the tomato paste," said Con.

"We don't have any choice, do we?" said Judy.

Once again I was smeared with the sticky red stuff. Judy then washed me with shampoo several times and finally, with no tomato paste remaining in the house, I was ready to emerge.

They toweled me off, then dried me with a hair dryer.

"What do you think?" asked Judy.

"I guess it's the best that we can do," said Con.

At that point, the smell around me was about at the level of a skunk roadkill. Pretty strong, pretty offensive, but not completely overpowering. You could stand next to me without clapping your hand over your mouth and looking for a toilet bowl.

"Pretty awful," said Con.

"Let's hope it wears off soon," said Judy.

At first, I couldn't smell anything. The secretions were so powerful that my sensitive nose gave up in disgust and refused to function.

Curiously enough, however, as my nose started to readjust, I sort of liked the smell. It lingered on for about ten days, fading bit by bit each day until it was finally gone. Con and Judy were quite happy that the smell disappeared so quickly, but I was a little sad. I liked smelling bad.

Here we have a curious quirk of dogs. Dogs like to wallow in things that smell bad to humans. Give a dog a ripe old carcass of something that's been dead too long, and the dog rushes forward and rolls in the smell, coming home as pleased as punch. Dogs like musky odors, they like acrid odors, and they like them at relatively high concentrations of smell, concentrations that are guaranteed to be offensive to humans.

Isn't this strange, you say. Here we have dogs with a sense of smell that might be a million times more sensitive than the sense of smell possessed by the average human, and still dogs like to roll in smells that gag most people. What is going on here?

For us, bad smells are like perfume is for people. In fact, perfume smells bad to us. Have you ever noticed what happens to all the dogs in a household when a heavily-perfumed guest comes to visit? The well-behaved, polite dogs simply find an excuse to be somewhere else in the house, where they don't have to put up with the stench. The less-well-behaved, less-polite, more-aggressive dogs might very well take a bite out of the visitor's leg, leaving the owner to mumble something like: that's really strange – he's never done anything like that before.

So why this difference? Perhaps it's not a difference at all. Think about what perfumes do for people. The normal unwashed person soon starts to smell of what, in polite society, is called body odor. This body odor, to sensitive noses at least, provides information about the individual identity of the human, the general mood, the gender, and the general hormonal state of each person. Con says that scientific experiments have shown that humans are sensitive to these odors, even if they don't realize it on a day-to-day level. One experiment showed that wives could pick out their husbands' dirty t-shirts from a crowd of other shirts owned by strange males, just by sniffing each shirt. Washing with soap and using deodorants disguises these odors, making it difficult for other people to tell what someone's mood or reproductive status really is. And using perfumes further disguises this, by swamping the nose with strong odors.

Dogs are exactly the same, just different. For exactly the same reasons, we occasionally like to disguise our natural smells, so that the bully down the street can't smell the fear that surrounds us whenever he appears. And, since our noses are so much more sensitive than human noses, we need a much stronger smell to disguise our own odors. A weak smell can still let other odor molecules punch through. A strong smell incapacitates all the nasal receptors. To us, human perfumes are weak smells, and mixed in with the normal human smells, produce a nauseating combination. To people, our perfumes are enough to gag a maggot.

So I was less than happy to see my acquired smell disappear. Con and Judy, however, were ecstatic, and for many months, Con would shine a light around the entire run at night before he would let me go down the stairs.

Such is the power of smell in controlling the behavior of humans.

Freedom

P oodles are hunting dogs. When we see something move, our genetic program kicks in and we're off in a flash.

Judy and I were taking a walk in a part of the woods where we had never been before. She was working with me off leash, letting me go away from her, then calling me back. I thought that was a great game, and was willing to go along with it. After all, it seemed to make her happy.

Then it happened! I felt a delicious smell wafting through the air. An elk! And close, too! I was off in a flash.

"Zephyr! Zephyr! Come!" I could hear Judy yelling.

My mind, however, was yelling, Elk! Elk!

I raced forward, and could just get a glimpse of the elk. If I just could put on a burst of speed, maybe I could catch up with it. Not that I wanted to kill it or anything like that. I just wanted to prove my prowess as a hunter. Not many dogs could say that they caught up with a wild elk in the woods!

I put on a burst of speed. So did the elk.

We ran for about ten minutes, with me barely gaining, but beginning to catch up. Then the elk put on another burst of speed, made a quick turn, and was gone.

I ran around, smelling, trying to catch the scent. No elk!

Where could that animal have gone? It's not so easy to hide an elk in the woods, particularly from a sensitive nose. Still no elk!

Okay, I knew when to concede defeat. The elk outwitted me, a hard realization for a poodle. Time to find Judy.

Then I realized what I had done. The elk and I had been running at about 30 miles per hour for about ten minutes. That meant that I had traveled about, let's see, how many miles? And where was Judy?

I looked around. Nothing was familiar. Small wonder. I had never been here before. All the trees looked the same.

Maybe if I smelled, perhaps I could smell either Judy or her car. But, no luck. Nothing but woods smell.

Perhaps if I listened. Judy was sure to be yelling for me.

But again, no luck. Nothing but woods sounds.

Then I started to get frightened. We had driven about 20 miles from town to get here, and the woods go on in all directions for about another 20-30 miles. How was I going to find Judy? Panic filled my brain, and I flopped down on the ground, panting.

Judy, meanwhile, ran after me as I ran after the elk, but a human can't run very fast. She lost sight of me in less than two seconds. So, she tried walking in the same direction in which I had disappeared, yelling for me at the top of her lungs.

As she wandered around, she managed to get lost. In the woods, all directions look alike, and the sun was practically overhead, so she couldn't try to estimate which direction she had come. Now, both of us were lost.

I lay on the ground for a while, trying to catch my breath and listening. Nothing! No Judy.

Then a thought crossed my mind. For the first time in my life, I was free. There were no humans around to catch me by my collar and discipline me. No one was going to tell me what to do. No one was going to put me on a leash. I could go where I wanted, when I wanted, and do whatever I pleased.

You can't imagine how satisfying it felt, to realize that I was free. We dogs live in a kind of serfdom, giving up our freedom for the privilege of being fed and having a roof over our heads. Yes, it is nice to be stroked, and fed, and cared for, but do we really need it?

I thought about it for a while. I realized that I could just get up and begin to live my own life. Sure, that meant hunting, but I was bred for hunting, it was in my genes. I was pretty confident that I could survive in the wild. Sure, that meant not getting any strokes, but instead I would have freedom. Did I want to live in a gilded cage, or did I want to live as free as the wind?

I thought of Judy and Con. Were they my masters, keeping me in a gilded cage? Or were they my friends? Really, they were both masters and friends. And what would they do without me? Who would make sure that they got their daily exercise? Who would make sure that they got a constant stream of love?

And what about Seri the cat? Who would make sure that she got chased all over the house?

I realized that I had responsibilities. Yes, it would be nice to be free, but the emotional cost was too immense. Judy and Con loved me, and I loved them. I couldn't just abandon them. I had to go back.

Getting back was something of a problem, however. I had a general sense of the direction that I had taken when I ran after the elk, but no specific sense of the distance. Nor did I know where Judy was.

I decided to try to head out in the general direction from which I had come. I hoped that I hadn't made too many turns in running after the elk, and that the general direction would eventually put me in the vicinity of the dirt road on which we had come from town.

My muscles were sore after such a flat-out run, but I knew that Judy was probably frantic, and I wanted to find her as quickly as possible. I ran as fast as I could, stopping every quarter mile or so to listen and smell. Nothing – no sounds of people, no smells of people. Time stretched out into half-an-hour, then even longer. Still nothing.

Then, off in the distance, I heard the high-pitched whine of a car. That must be the road! I put on a burst of speed.

Judy was still lost. She kept calling,

"Zephyr! Zephyr! Where are you? Come!"

By now her voice had gotten hoarse. Almost an hour had gone by, with no dog in sight.

Finally, she came across an old logging track, barely visible among the forest litter. She reasoned that the track had to go toward the road, if only she could pick the right direction. Mentally she flipped a coin, and decided to go to her left along the track. She walked for about ten minutes, and finally heard a car in the distance. She was no longer lost! The road was somewhere ahead of her.

I ran toward the road, and finally there it was, the dirt road. Now, where was Judy, where was the car? I started to smell, and my nose picked up the faint smell of Judy's car. I ran in that direction, and perhaps a quarter of a mile away, there was the car. Not too bad a piece of navigation for a lost poodle! But where was Judy?

Judy came out on the dirt road, and again had to mentally flip a coin to decide which direction to take. She had no idea where her car was in relation to where the logging track joined the road. And, the road was traveled by cars, but not all that often. Perhaps one car per hour, on average, used that road. At that rate, she could walk quite a distance in the wrong direction before she could flag down a car on the road and ask for a ride to her car.

She decided to turn right this time. She walked along the road, still calling:

"Zephyr! Where are you? Come!" Now her voice was barely a whisper.

Around a turn, there was the car. She wasn't lost anymore.

As she started to walk toward the car, I emerged from behind the fender. I was a little bit hesitant to come up to her, because I didn't know what she would do. Humans are sometimes unpredictable. I've seen a mother spank her kid because she was relieved that the kid didn't get hit by a car when the kid ran out into the street. Would Judy do the same to me?

But Judy was so overjoyed to see me, she sat down into the dirt of the road, threw her arms around my neck and started to sob. I was glad to see her too, and started to whimper. It's a good thing that the road was traveled so infrequently. We must have been sitting in the middle of the road for about fifteen minutes, crying. Finally, we got into the car and left.

Although I lost my chance at a life in the wild, I'm glad I made the decision to go back. My humans need me, perhaps more than I need them. That in itself is freedom.

Dog School

P oodles are social dogs. We like to be around people, and we like
to be around other dogs. Some of us think that we are people,
and others of us would never dream of stooping so low.

Even though I saw other dogs on my walks, Con and Judy decided
that I needed to be around other dogs in a more structured situation.
This translates as obedience lessons in a formal class. Con thought
that I would lose some of my natural exuberance toward other dogs if I
could be somewhere where all the dogs were well-behaved. Naturally,
I took a rather dim view of this opinion. I thought that I was perfectly
well-behaved toward other dogs, and if I wanted to drill on command
with a bunch of other dogs, I would have joined the army.

However, I had no say in the matter. I was trundled off to an obedience class, taught by a trainer who had been working with dogs for as
long as anyone could remember. He claimed that he could understand
the motivation of any breed of dog, under any circumstances.

"OK, everyone line up here, with your dog next to you," he yelled
in a drill-instructor's voice.

People and dogs started shuffling around. There were St. Bernards, there were Akitas, there were Jack Russell Terriers, and there was a Pomeranian, to name just a few of the participants. It seemed to me that the bigger the dog, the smaller the owner. The two St. Bernards were both held by women who weighed less than 90 pounds and stood less than five feet high. Conversely, the Pomeranian was with a beefy, 250 pound, six-foot-four-inch-tall man, who was given moral support by his beefy, 200 pound, six-foot-tall wife.

Very quickly, chaos ensued. Some dogs drifted off toward the left of their owners, other dogs moved toward their owner's right side, and other dogs simply managed to wrap their leashes around their owners' legs.

"No, no, no!" yelled the instructor. "Dogs on the left, people on the right!"

I thought this meant that all the dogs could go off together toward the left of the practice arena, while the people had to stay together on the right. But no, it was not to be.

Some of the people were confused too. They started to move in random directions, with the inevitable result that several dogs got themselves and their owners tangled up with the leashes of other dogs.

"No, no, no!" yelled the instructor. "No contact with other dogs!"

"Why not?" asked Con.

The instructor looked at Con as though Con had just asked the stupidest question in the world.

"Dogs can bite," he said.

"Yes, but they can learn how to socialize with one another," Con said.

"Dogs can bite," said the instructor, with a dismissive air.

"No biting in class!"

Finally, everyone got sorted out. People and dogs stood in a line abreast, with each dog on the left of each person.

"Today we will learn how to sit!" yelled the instructor. Most of the people looked very impressed.

"Sit!" the instructor yelled at the dogs.

No one budged. I knew the command and what was expected of me, but I was not about to cooperate at this point. I only glanced with some reproach at Con, thinking, how could you have gotten me into this?

The instructor approached a dog, pushed down on the animal's hind end, and gave the dog's collar a yank. The dog sat.

"Sit!" said the instructor triumphantly.

Now all the other people started to tentatively push on the hind ends of their dogs and tug at the dogs' collars. Dogs and people started dancing around, with some people ending up on the ground in a sitting position with their dogs standing over them.

"No, no, no!" yelled the trainer. "The dogs sit, not the people!"

At that point, an Akita started acting up, trying to get to another dog and practically pulling its owner off his feet in the process. The Akita wasn't trying to be vicious – he was just bored and wanted to socialize with another dog.

The trainer saw all this out of the corner of his eye. A grim tight-lipped smile crossed his face. He ran up to the Akita, grabbed the leash, and WHACK! WHACK! gave the leash two tugs that practically caused the dog to lose his balance.

"Gotta show them who's boss," said the trainer. "You let 'em act up, and pretty soon they run away."

"And what do you do when they run away?" asked Con.

"As soon as they come back, you wallop them over the head with a stick. That'll teach 'em," said the trainer.

That taught Con that we were in the wrong class. As soon as we could gracefully slip away, we left, never to return to that trainer. I thought about what the trainer had said. How would you like to come back to your person, only to have him hit you on the head with a stick? Wouldn't that encourage you to run away again and, this time, stay away?

But Con had not given up on the idea of enrolling me in an organized obedience class. Soon he found another trainer, one who obviously liked the dogs in her classes. She did not believe in hitting the dogs, with a stick or with anything else. She was firm but patient. I liked her a lot.

We went through six weeks of classes, and I once again went through all the commands I already knew – Sit, Down, Stay, Heel, Come. In a way, it was kind of fun in her class. The dogs all enjoyed themselves, and there was a lot of snickering when an owner would mess up and forget how to do a command. Since people are notoriously hard to train, that kind of thing happened fairly often.

Finally came graduation day. We were all competing for first place. The object was to see which dog could respond to all the commands flawlessly, then go on a Down-Stay, wait for the owner to say "Come," then come up to the owner and sit down in front of the person.

Con was sure that I would take first place. I already knew all the commands. I am a smart dog. He thought that he and I were going to get the blue ribbon, hands down.

When my turn came, I did all the commands flawlessly. I went on a Down-Stay and waited. Everything was really sharp. Everyone was very impressed. Then Con said, "Come". I got up quickly and quickly ran to Con. And I kept going. And going. And going.

"Zephyr, come back!" said Con, in an embarrassed tone of voice.

Everyone started laughing.

"Zephyr, come back, NOW!" yelled Con.

I ran up to Con and jumped away just as he reached for my collar. Then I started to run rings around him.

By now, we were the main stage and complete center of attention. The trainer was just standing there – her professionalism kept her from laughing. No one else felt the least bit professional. Everyone was roaring.

Con was getting redder and redder. His embarrassment was rapidly being replaced with high blood pressure.

"Zephyr, I mean it!" he yelled.

I could see that if I kept this up for too long, he would have a stroke or something. I stopped, trotted over to him, and sat down in the exact position I should have used after the "Come" command, facing him. Everyone clapped.

Needless to say, I finished last. Even the dogs that could barely remember the commands got a higher score.

As we were walking toward the car, Con turned to me and said,

"Zephyr, how could you do this? You knew those commands! What got into you?"

Pal, I said, I know your competitive spirit. If I had done a perfect job, you would have been so proud of me that you would have wanted me to compete in dog shows. I just wanted to show you what would happen if you ever tried to exploit me to satisfy your pride.

"Zephyr," said Con, "if I believed in hitting dogs, I would paddle a poodle. It's a good thing for you that I don't believe that dogs should be hit, under any circumstances. But just for that, we're going to take you to a dog show. You don't have to compete, but you jolly well are going to watch and see how your betters do things."

Whoopie, a dog show. Not what I always wanted to see. But I consoled myself with fantasies of smuggling Seri in and releasing her during the judging when all the dogs are neatly lined up, waiting for the judge to decide who is the top dog.

DOG SHOW

I can't say that I was thrilled about going to a dog show. The thought of all those dogs prancing around for approval made me slightly sick to my stomach. But, as so often happens, I had no choice in the matter. At least no one had any immediate plans to make ME prance around in front of a crowd.

As we drove up to the parking lot of the field where the dog show was being held, Con said, "Zephyr, I want you to pay attention to what those dogs are doing. I want you to be as obedient as they when we ask you to obey."

Not very likely, I thought.

Con parked the car, put on my harness, and away we went. To make sure that I behaved well, Con put a Gentle Leader leash on me. The basic principle is that as the dog surges forward, the leash, which is attached to a harness that fits over the dog's muzzle, pulls the head downward. This slows down the surging dog, and at the same time, the head moving downward is a signal of submission. With one gentle leash pull, you have a submissive, well-behaved dog. I have never liked this leash. Having something fit over my nose is bad enough. But having my nose pulled downward is even worse. I must admit, however, that it works just like it was designed – it keeps dogs from pulling or getting too excited.

Dogs were everywhere. Big dogs, small dogs, lapdogs, yapdogs. Most of them were inside portable wire cages next to the vans and RVs that had brought them. Some dogs were being exercised by their owners. An air of tension and excitement filled the place.

We walked inside the fence where the judging was taking place. I was on my best behavior. Not only was the Gentle Leader keeping me from doing anything, but the whole atmosphere of obedience seemed to have sunk into my muscles. I wanted to look good in front of the other dogs.

"Hi, what kind of leash is that?" said a man near one of the arenas. Con put on his I-am-lecturing voice.

"This is a Gentle Leader. It is a painless and gentle way of controlling a dog's behavior. It is particularly good for aggressive dogs, but can be used for any type of dog, because it uses natural dog behavior to make the dog do what you want, painlessly and quickly."

Come on, Con. I was embarrassed. Why doesn't Con simply say, "a Gentle Leader" and walk on? In my embarrassment, I almost missed what the man was now saying.

"I train dogs, and I've found that pain is good for them. A good quick snap of the choker teaches them who's boss. Snap their heads off a few times, and they learn. I get really quick results that way." In other words, I interpreted, I like to get really macho with dogs and make them hurt.

Con started to bristle.

"This is a completely painless way of controlling the dog. You don't need to snap anyone's head off this way. Besides, you could permanently injure a dog by snapping a choker too hard."

"You just have to know how to do it. You snap it up here."

He reached down toward my neck and showed an area just behind my skull.

"That causes the most pain, and you don't injure the dog."

I started eyeing the man's leg, and wondering if I could get away with biting him. No, I sadly concluded. The Gentle Leader didn't let me open up my mouth wide enough to sink my teeth in. Too bad.

Con's blood pressure was rising quickly.

"There's no need to do that. Why don't you try doing it without hurting the dog?"

I can tell you why, I thought. The man likes to hurt things. This is why he works with dogs – it gives him a chance to bully an animal, to inflict his rage and pain on a living creature. The more the animal fights him, the more he likes it. He can beat the dog into a pulp, all in the name of training. Completely acceptable socially.

Con opened his mouth for a scathing rebuttal. I started to sneeze.

"Zephyr, what's the matter?" said Con.

Sneeze, sneeze, sneeze, sneeze.

"Excuse me," said Con to the bully, and took me away from the arena.

I had accomplished what I had set out to do – I got Con out of an argument. I knew perfectly well that there was no way that Con could convince the bully that people should be kind, gentle, and nice to their dogs. The man had probably been hurting dogs for years and would continue to hurt dogs until someone got him into court for cruelty to animals. You either feel an empathy for animals, or you don't. People are hard to change.

We started to walk around to the different arenas. I had a chance to look at some of the dogs and some of their owners.

Most of the dogs were really excited. They liked being at the show. They liked seeing other dogs. They liked competing.

Many of the owners were really tense. To them, it was vital that THEIR dog wins. They feel a sense of personal triumph when their dog gets a ribbon. They also feel a sense of personal failure when their dog does not get enough points to place. They are willing to endlessly groom their dogs, to train with them, to practice, practice, practice.

I thought, what a tragedy. Wouldn't it be better if these obedience trials were held just for people? Leave the dogs out of it. Just let the people compete against one another – see who can sit fastest, who remembers how to do a figure 8 with the most precision, and so forth. Just leave the "middle man," the dog, out of the picture entirely.

But then I realized that a dog show catered to two human foibles: control and besting one's peers. Humans seem to like to impose their will on other living creatures (they would probably also like to impose their will on non-living creatures, but there is kind of an unsatisfying lack of response in making a table "heel"). They like to make other people do their bidding. Often this is couched in the social conventions of morality, ethics, religion, politics, and social conformity. The operating principle seems to be: I can prove to myself that I am more powerful than you if I can make you do what I want. Human history can be summed up as the search for control.

The other foible, besting one's peers, is really a subset of the control issue. The operating principle here is: If I can best all my peers, they will realize that I am more powerful than they, and they will let me control their behavior. Power comes with the control. The more powerful you are, the more you can control other people's behavior.

Conversely, the more you can control other people's behavior, the more powerful you are.

And the game of control gets transferred from human social inter- action to interactions with dogs at dog shows. This way, people can exert their control over others (dogs) and, at the same time, best their peers (other dog owners). In a way, it is a surrogate for the real game of human social interactions, sort of like chess is a surrogate for real war.

So by now, do you think that I am looking down my nose at dog shows and human control? No. Dogs like to do it too. We dogs have dominance hierarchies, which are about control and power. More dominant dogs can control the behavior of subordinates and can get access to more of the resources: food, affection, whatever. In fact, I realized at the dog show that besting-one's-peers also applied to the dogs. They liked to win. They liked the dominance, the status, that came from winning. Most of the dogs could no longer interact with other pack members (in fact, some show dog owners will not even let their dogs play with other dogs, in case the coat of the dog gets soiled), so this was a way of playing the dominance-control game in another setting. The people got their dominance, status, and power through their dogs. And the dogs got their dominance, status, and power through their people, by having their people bring them to shows.

Humans and dogs both seem to have an instinctive love for control and power. Perhaps that is one reason we dogs allowed ourselves to be domesticated, and now we can control humans sometimes.

BOARDING

For several days, the activity of the household had intensified. Con and Judy were rushing around, cleaning up the house, watering the plants, and paying the bills. I watched all this, wondering what had gotten into them.

Finally, Con hauled out some suitcases.

"Zephyr," said Judy with a touch of guilt in her voice, "we're going to have to take you to a kennel. But don't worry. We'll be back for you before you know it!"

Frankly, I doubted anyone could do something before I knew it, but I was willing to let that slide as I pondered a more pressing question: what in the world was a kennel?

"Con, do you have Zephyr's blanket, and a pad that he can use for a bed?" asked Judy.

"Yes, and I also have his favorite toy."

"Good. I'll cook up some of the meat that he likes to be added to his food, and we'll put that into a bunch of plastic bags so that the kennel people can add that to his food each time they feed him."

Seri was watching all this activity with a sad expression. She knew from previous experience that she was going to be left alone in the house, with a neighbor coming by once a day to feed her and clean her litterbox. Since Seri didn't like or trust other people, that meant that every time the neighbor came by, Seri would hide under the bed, missing out on the cuddles and strokes that she felt she needed daily from her people. Con explained to me much later on that cats really are more social than most people think. When housecats live in a semi-wild state, such as in barns on farms, they live in social groups, with closely related females sleeping next to one another. The idea that cats are totally self-sufficient and completely aloof from humans is a myth, probably started by humans who have never been around cats very much.

"Zephyr, you'll like this kennel," said Judy. "It's really very nice. We checked it out very carefully before we made a reservation for you. They have large dog runs that have an inside compartment where you can sleep and an outside part where you can run around and enjoy the fresh air. And the inside compartment has heating coils embedded in the floor so that you won't get cold at night."

OK, I thought, but why are we all moving to a kennel?

Con loaded my stuff into the car and got me inside. Judy patted me on the head, told me that she loved me and that she'll miss me. At that point, I realized that I was the only one going to this kennel. I was bitterly disappointed that my people would do this to me! Con explained to me that he and Judy had to go to a conference in another state and that they would be gone for a week. He carefully pointed out to me that I shouldn't worry, that they would come back for me and that I was supposed to view my time in the kennel as a way of relaxing and getting to know other dogs.

At the kennel, Con handed over my leash to the attendant, who took me into another room. Barking all around me exploded in a cacophony of sound! There were deep barks, little yaps, and voices in between, all straining to produce the loudest bark. It was deafening. I must admit, it was sort of scary. What sort of place was this, and what did they do to poodles here?

The attendant took off my leash as he put me into a large dog run. Then he came back with my blanket, bed, and toy, and put those into the run with me. Now I was alone, in the company of what seemed like hundreds of other dogs, all barking their fool heads off.

I started looking around me. In the run next to me were a German Shepherd and a Collie. In the other run, on the other side, was a Rottweiler. Across the narrow hall, I could see a couple of small runs with a Miniature Poodle and a Schnauser. At least the Poodle made me feel better. Apparently, they don't eat poodles for lunch here, I thought.

Hi, my name is Zephyr. I'm a Standard Poodle, I said politely to the couple on one side.

Hi, I'm George, said the German Shepherd.

And I'm Sally, said the Collie. We live in the same house, so when we go to the kennel, we stay in the same run. It's cheaper for our people, and we like being together.

So you've been to a kennel before? I asked.

Oh, yes, many times, said Sally. Our people are always going somewhere. This is like a second home for us.

Yes, said George. It's kind of fun, in a way. We get to meet other dogs and talk about all sorts of things. We can swap stories about our people and their crazy antics. You won't believe some of the stories the dogs here have to tell! If this is your first time in a kennel, I guarantee that you'll learn things about people that will make your hair curl!

My hair was already curled, but I was born that way. I was fascinated with the prospect of learning more about what it's like being a dog.

It's not all fun and games, mind you, said Sally. We miss our people, and we miss the contact with humans. The people here are very nice, but no one comes in to stroke you or to play fetch with you. In that respect, it can get very boring. Also, sometimes it can be your bad luck to get stuck next to some tedious bores who drone on and on about some pet topic, without listening or caring about what YOU have to say on the matter. We were stuck one time next to a Cocker Spaniel whose favorite topic was fleas. She went on and on about how her flea bites itched, how her people tried her out on different flea collars and dips, and how she hated the collars and the dips. After a whole week of that, we were ready to howl at just the mere mention of a flea!

Say, you're not stuck on fleas, are you? asked George.

Not at all, I hastened to assure them. I have no interest in fleas. I prefer to talk about philosophy. Say, who do you think is smarter, people or cats?

This provoked an hour of serious discussion. George thought that people were smarter, by a slim margin. Sally thought that the honors went to cats, hands down. Sally thought that just because people could talk, you couldn't assume that they were truly intelligent. Her position was that people were mostly ruled by emotions, while cats used clear logic in manipulating their humans into taking care of the cats. George argued that people can sometimes be intelligent on an individual basis, although there was scant evidence of that when all of humanity was pooled as a group, and there was usually no evidence of that when people interacted with their dogs. However, he was willing to give some humans the benefit of the doubt and talked about how some humans had the potential to be intelligent, even though they wasted this potential most of the time. Both George and Sally were in agreement that neither people nor cats could touch dogs in the smarts department.

So how do you really know that humans aren't very intelligent? I asked.

Well, think about it, said Sally. They can't smell worth beans, they can't hear worth anything, it's hard for us to teach them tricks, and they spend large portions of each day doing meaningless things that don't seem to make them very happy. How can anyone like that be intelligent?

I acknowledged that she had a point there.

Excuse me, said George, but all this talk has made me hungry. He wandered off in search of his food dish.

In the meanwhile, the Rottweiler had drifted over and stuck his nose into the wire mesh near where I was standing.

Hello, my name is Zephyr.

"Woof," said the Rottweiler.

Pardon me? I asked. A "woof" was not very informative in dog conversation.

Don't bother, said Sally. He's a sad case. Can't talk. His people took him away from his mom and his litter when he was only four weeks old before he learned to speak. As a result, not only can he not talk, but he's pretty aggressive to dogs and people, too. He doesn't know how to socialize with either group and is kind of afraid of any person or dog he encounters, so he lashes out with his teeth. Not a very pretty picture.

So why would his people take him away from his mom when he was only four weeks old? Didn't they know any better? I asked.

Apparently not, said Sally. I heard some of the attendants here talking about it. The male owner is one of these know-it-all types—been around dogs all his life, knows everything, you can't tell him anything. His wife called in a behavioral expert once to see what the problem was. The expert apparently explained that the dog was not properly socialized and that four weeks was too early to take a dog out of a litter. The man sneered at this, then spent the next two months telling his wife and anyone else who would listen about how he knew more about dogs than behaviorists with Ph.Ds.! Like I was saying, humans aren't very intelligent!

As time passed, life settled down into a routine for me. I would wake up, greet the new day by running around, then settle down to talk with George and Sally. Eventually, we would all get sleepy in the heat of the day and curl up for naps. Then dinnertime, and then time for bed. I missed Con and Judy, and I missed my walks, but all told, life in the kennel was not too bad.

One afternoon I was sound asleep when the kennel person came in and took my leash and harness off the hook. I sprang up as all the dogs started barking.

Well, pal, said George, looks like it's time for you to go. They always do that when your owner arrives.

I was so excited that I started to leap in my run. Going home! I'm going home!

The kennel person opened the door, put on my harness, and snapped on my leash.

Bye, guys! was all I had time to say as I surged toward the door. The door opened, and there was Con!

"Hi, Zephyr! Did you have a good time here?" said Con.

Come on, Con! Get me home!

As we were driving back in the car, I thought about my time in the kennel. I enjoyed talking to some of the dogs and learning about their lives. So was it really terrible to be in the kennel? On balance, no. So do I want to go back to a kennel? On balance, no. I had an OK time, but it wasn't home, and I wanted to be home! Even seeing Seri again looked pretty good just now!

A Greyhound Friend

O ne morning Con and Judy got up early and started packing a
suitcase.

Oh-oh, I thought, does that mean that I have to go to a kennel?

Seeing my worried look, Con told me, "Relax, Zephyr. We're going
for a ride, to Judy's cousin's house. There you're going to meet her
dog, a greyhound called Sam. You'll have a great time playing with
one another, and we're going to stay there overnight, so you'll have a
lot of time to spend with him."

The last part worried me. What if I didn't like Sam? I had heard
about greyhounds, but didn't know any personally. Someone had told
me that greyhounds run pretty fast, but beyond that I had no idea
what a greyhound was as a dog.

But then, as an optimistic poodle, I wasn't about to worry. I would
take things one step at a time, and the first step was, I was going for a
ride!

I have been riding in a car for almost my entire life. Con and Judy
brought me home in a car when I was eight weeks old, and since that

time I've gotten out for a ride almost every day. Let me tell you, I love to go for rides. I love to watch the scenery. I love to smell the scents. Next to going for a walk, a ride is one of the major high points of life.

Con and Judy had some rules of the road. On a ride, I was supposed to sit in the back seat. Personally, I would have preferred to drive. I am convinced that I would have done better at driving than Con or Judy, who tend to drive too slowly and cautiously. Give me the wheel and the gas pedal, and I'd be there in no time! The only problem is that I can't reach the gas pedal, but why worry about trifles?

The sitting was supposedly for the sake of safety. As I was starting to grow, Con and Judy had a series of discussions about how to ensure that I would be safe if they brake suddenly or if another car hit us. Con wanted to put me into a harness attached to the rear seatbelt, so we went to various pet shops and tried various harnesses. None of them was designed for the large chest of a poodle, and none seemed to attach very well to the rear seatbelt. Each time we tried on a harness, I felt like I was trussed up in a fishing net. Finally, Con and Judy settled on teaching me to sit and forgetting about the harness. Now I sit most of the time, usually in the space between the two front seats – I'm still in the back, mind you, but I'm so large that I can lean my head forward so that part of my body is exactly between Con and Judy. That way, I can pretend I'm driving and mentally give advice to Con or Judy as they drive.

For some reason, my sitting between Con and Judy seems to puzzle other drivers. One day, Con was driving, and I was pretending that I was driving in the Indy 500, when a car came zooming by on our right (I would have never let any car zoom past us if I were really driving!). The driver glanced at us, did a double-take, and almost lost control of the car. He slowed down, so that we got ahead, and then we had to stop at a red light (another thing that would not have stopped me if I were driving). The driver zoomed up next to us again, opened up his window, and he and his passenger stared at us.

"SEE, I TOLD you it was a dog and not a little kid!" said the man who was driving, looking triumphantly at the woman who was in the passenger seat. The woman looked very sour, ensuring that the man would probably pay dearly for his petty triumph.

Another rule of the road is that I can never stick my head or even my nose out the window when the car is moving. Con feels that there is too much chance of something hitting my face, a bug or a rock, for me to be able to do this. While I am sure he is right, it doesn't stop me from wishing I could occasionally ride with my head out the window.

A third rule is that when we stop and a door opens, I must remain sitting until Con or Judy tells me it's OK to jump out. As Con explained to me, this is for my own safety again. If something happened and Con and Judy had to get out of the car and left the door open, they didn't want me jumping out into traffic and possibly getting hit by a car.

So I was going for a ride. I ran around excitedly, jumping around and barking until finally I was in the car, and off we went.

"Zephyr, it's going to be a long trip, so I'd settle down if I were you," said Con.

The trip to Judy's cousin's house indeed turned out to be a long one as far as I was concerned – more than two hours. I pretended that I was driving for about the first hour, then got bored with Con's cautious driving and went to sleep on the back seat.

"Zephyr, wake up, we're here!" said Judy.

I was up in a flash, eager to see what a greyhound was when it was at home.

We went up to the door, and there waiting for us was a dog as big as me, but with almost no hair. Also, the dog wasn't grey, he was mostly brown.

We went through all the dog protocols of greeting, Sam and I. This meant, first we sniff noses, then each dog goes around and sniffs the behind of the other dog, where we dogs have anal glands. These glands tell us a lot of information about the other dog – the sex, the age, the general level of health, and the individual odor of the other dog, which we can later use to identify the dog when we smell that odor on poop or on furniture.

Sam turned out to be a nice dog, kind and gentle. We went out into the backyard to play. I was a little stiff from sleeping in the car, and Sam was eager to run. The backyard was relatively small but still big enough for a dog like me to build up a little bit of speed.

Did I tell you that I am a fast dog? I can run faster than just about any dog that I've been around, so I thought I could outrun Sam any day. I tore out toward the far fence while Sam was just standing there. Halfway there, Sam was still standing and watching me. Then suddenly there was a whoosh as something came rocketing along next to me, and the next thing I knew, Sam was still standing and watching me, but now he was standing at my destination, the far side of the fence. I had never seen a dog run that fast. I was impressed.

During the time I was with Sam, he told me something about his life as a greyhound. He was bred for the racetrack. Apparently, people raise greyhounds just so that the greyhounds can run in races and make money for these people. Other people come to the racetrack and bet money on the dogs, so for the greyhound breeders, having a fast dog is very important. The dogs live in small cages, without much human company. When they lie down in their cages, they have hard concrete to lie on and can wear off the fur on their hind legs from lying on the hard floor. The whole purpose of the dogs, as far as the people are concerned, is to win races. The dogs chase either an artificial rabbit or sometimes a real rabbit around the track, trying to run as fast as they can.

The dogs like to run, but the pressure on them to win is fierce. Since racing greyhounds is viewed as a business, sort of like canning sardines, a dog that doesn't run fast enough to win is a liability – it eats food, takes up space, and doesn't bring its owner an economic return.

Not too many years ago, dogs that didn't win were simply killed. It just wasn't profitable for the owners to keep them. Now, however, there are greyhound rescue organizations that take these dogs and try to find good homes for them. The rescue organizations try to make sure that a good home has people in it who know about the care and feeding of greyhounds, and that the people will be kind and gentle with these dogs.

Sam told me a little bit about what kind of dogs greyhounds are, and what kind of dogs greyhounds are not. They are dogs who like to run and chase things, so cats are not very safe around greyhounds. They also like to run for long distances, so they can't be taken out into the woods and allowed to run free. By the time they took stock of their bearings, they would have run many miles before realizing they'd gotten lost. They aren't very aggressive and don't bark very much, so they aren't very good guard dogs. They are reluctant to be trained to sit, lie down, and go through the other kinds of obedience things that dogs learn – it's not that they can't do it, it's just that they don't like to do it. They are, however, kind and gentle dogs, usually good with children, and full of love and affection.

Sam was a dog who couldn't win. No matter how hard he tried, he just couldn't run as fast as some of the other dogs, so he got kicked out of the racetrack circuit at the age of two. However, Sam turned out to be a winner thanks to a greyhound rescue group. He became a beloved dog in Judy's cousin's household, playmate and companion to two little kids who tore around the house racing toy cars while Sam placidly lay in the middle of all the commotion. He said that he sometimes wondered how he got so lucky to end up with such a wonderful family.

Unfortunately, Sam's good life was relatively short-lived. One day he and Judy's cousin were walking around their neighborhood when they came across two Rottweilers who were running loose without owner or leashes. The Rottweilers attacked both Sam and Judy's cousin, tearing into both of them and slashing with their teeth. A car stopped, and Judy's cousin managed to get Sam into the vehicle, with the Rottweilers still snapping and snarling. Sam was rushed to a nearby vet's office, where he underwent emergency surgery. Valiantly, he tried to recover. But the wounds were so extensive, and infection set in. He wanted so much to live. Instead, he died.

CHASING DEER

Con is not entirely hopeless about letting me off my leash. Some days the weather is gorgeous, the wind is blowing a gentle breeze, the temperature is balmy, and Con starts to feel at peace with himself. On those days, I know that he will be confident enough about me to let me run free.

One such day he and I were walking in the woods when a herd of deer ran out in front of us. I should have smelled them, but I was busy nosing around in gopher burrows, and my nose was somewhat out of commission from the strong musty smells of both the gophers and their burrows. Gophers like to dig under the roots of plants, and then pull the plants down into their burrows so that they can dine on the plants in relative privacy from predators. As a result, their burrows smell of decaying vegetation, with a strong component of gopher poop thrown in.

Four deer ran past us in a flash. I knew that I shouldn't betray Con's trust by chasing them, but something primal kicked in, and before I knew what I was doing, I was chasing them at full speed.

The deer were scared. I looked like a big, fierce predator, and I could run pretty fast. I started to gain on them.

Con started to yell, "Zephyr, come back here!" But I was caught up in the thrill of the chase.

The deer saw that I was gaining and started an escape maneuver. Later on, Con told me that this was a standard move for prey trying to escape from a predator. If the prey see that the predator is gaining, they try a turning strategy, where they start zig-zagging as they run. The idea here is that if they weigh less than the predator, each zig-zig will put more force during the turn on the predator than on the prey, making the predator lose ground. The principle is the same as when you go around a turn in your car. As the car turns, you sway in the opposite direction of the turn. If you were running, this sway would cause you to drift away from the road or your prey. Highway engineers know about such forces and build roads so that they are banked – otherwise, there would be a collection of wrecked cars at every turn. Prey use this principle to cause the predator to drift away from them and lose ground. Eventually, the predator tires out, and the prey get away. Unfortunately for the deer, I weighed about as much as they did, and I could keep up with them on their turns, gaining ground because I was running fast.

As I ran, I was admiring the supple grace of the deer, the way that they seemed to float effortlessly through the air, jumping over bushes, rarely touching their feet down on the ground. For what seemed like endless time, the deer and I were locked into sailing through the air, with bushes and rocks streaming by in a dazzling blur.

I didn't want to hurt the deer. I wasn't hungry. I didn't want to eat them. If the chase had ended right there, if the deer had stopped and stood there, I probably would have gone up to them, nuzzled them, and wanted to make friends. But while they were running, I was caught up in an instinctive need to catch up, to chase anything that was moving in front of me. My genes were in charge, and my brain was in neutral, experiencing the joy of the chase, the joy that must have kept generations of my ancestors alive as they chased down their prey.

I pulled up alongside the slowest deer. My instincts said, bite! Bite, grab, and hold on! This is how my wolf ancestors subdued their large prey. The first wolf to reach the prey bit, held on, and added his weight to the running prey animal. If he (or she) could hold on long enough, other wolves from the pack would come running up and would also bite. With four or five wolves holding on, the prey animal would not be able to keep on running and would be pulled to a stop. Then the wolves would tear their prey apart into little bits. My instinct said, this is what you are supposed to do! Bite!

But I wasn't a wolf, nor was I a dog ruled entirely by instincts. Most of the time I thought about what I was doing, and this time was no exception when it came to my genes telling me to bite. I controlled the urge and kept on running for the thrill of the chase.

The deer were starting to tire and were getting frantic. I could smell their fear. I could see that they thought they would lose somebody from their herd. I could hear their anguish and desperation in the way that they gulped in huge breaths of air.

And I wasn't interested in hurting them. While my genes caused me to start the chase, all that Zephyr, the thinking dog, wanted was to test his strength, to see if he could catch up to them. And he could. And that was enough.

I broke off the chase, turned around, and ran back toward where a frantic and angry Con was still yelling for me to come.

When I came back, Con's first instinct was to yell at me. However, he stopped himself just in time, praising me instead for returning to him. I was really proud of him, proud that he remembered that you can't yell at a dog that comes back to you.

I tried to explain to him that chasing moving animals is just part of my genes.

"Zephyr," said Con, "you can't use that excuse. You should be able to think of what you are doing and think of the consequences. You could have gotten lost!"

And humans stop to think of the consequences, was my thought. Humans have some of these instincts too, in my opinion. A strong instinct is the response to being chased. When I am in the car with Con and Judy, I always notice what happens when Con starts to pass a car on the highway. The car ahead of Con has been traveling slowly, so Con swings out into the left lane and starts to pass. Almost invariably, the car ahead suddenly puts on a burst of speed, moving as if it were being chased by some fierce predator. I'll be willing to bet that this is instinct kicking in. I'll also be willing to bet that the drivers of these cars don't even notice what they are doing – they don't stop to think.

Another instinct that I have noticed in humans is the hunting instinct. Human males particularly seem to enjoy various expressions of this instinct. Some males like to play ball – football, baseball, basketball. What is ball playing other than an expression of hunting, an expression of throwing things with some degree of accuracy at imaginary prey?

We dogs do the same thing. We love to chase sticks. Once we get the sticks, we love to run around with them, pretending that we are holding on to the rib-bone of an elk or a deer. If we are lucky enough to be able to play with other dogs off-leash, we love to run around with our imaginary rib-bones and play keep away, trying to keep the other dogs from taking the stick away from us. And how is that different from a game of football or basketball? A bunch of men run around the field without their leashes, trying to keep the ball away from other men.

The one expression of the hunting instinct that I can't understand in humans is going out and killing animals. I suppose I could understand it if these humans were starving and needed to eat – we dogs have had to do that for much of our history, just as most humans have had to do that as well. But in the days of corner supermarkets filled with shelves groaning with an abundance of meat, your average human hunter doesn't have to go out and shoot an animal to keep the family from starving. Some hunters shoot animals for sport, for the trophy, and for the excitement of the kill. Raw instinct, I would say. But as I think back to those magnificent deer that I was chasing, and think of their heads stuffed and mounted above the mantelpiece of some hunter, I feel a sadness that some humans can't rise above their instincts and appreciate the beauty of animals without needing to kill them.

RAJA

One fine day Con got a phone call from a lady who was having problems with her dogs. Did I tell you that Con helps people solve their problems with their pets? So he went off to see what the problem was.

When he arrived, he found that the lady had a pack of eight dogs, all running loose around her property.

"What seems to be the problem?" asked Con.

The lady, Beverly, replied, "I have a black poodle, Raja, who is a trouble-maker. He picks fights with all the other dogs, and I don't know what to do about him."

Con found the black poodle, who was very friendly and came up to him right away. The dog needed grooming and had scars on his body from the bites of other dogs. After watching the interactions of the other dogs with Raja, Con determined that the dominance hierarchy was unstable. All of the other dogs were beating up on the poodle.

He suggested to Beverly that the way to solve her problem was to find another home for Raja. Beverly readily agreed, and Con started to look for someone to adopt Raja. He tried some friends who were looking for a dog as a playmate for their eight-year-old daughter, but when Con's friend Bill went to look at Raja, Raja kept nipping at Bill's heels. Bill said a polite thanks but no thanks. Con tried rescue organizations, but everyone said they had no room.

Finally, Judy suggested that she and Con take Raja for an afternoon to evaluate how easy it would be to do obedience training with him, who at the age of two was totally untrained. Judy reasoned that if Raja could be trained in the basic commands, this would be an important selling point for someone to adopt him.

Con arranged with Beverly that she would bring Raja into town, to the parking lot of a large store, where Judy and Con could work a little bit with Raja and see how quickly he would learn some basic commands. Beverly showed up with a ragged Raja. The fur on his face almost completely covered his eyes. His foot pads had so much fur between them that he could hardly walk.

Judy put a harness on Raja and snapped a leash on it. Beverly stood by, crying. Judy asked why she was so sad.

"I hate to give up my dog, but it's for the best. Goodbye Raja, goodbye."

Judy was stunned. She said, "Wait a minute, we just agreed to take Raja for the afternoon."

"No, it can't work that way," sobbed Beverly. "He's your problem now."

With that, she got into her car and left. Con and Judy were left holding Raja's leash and holding their mouths open.

"What do we do now?" asked Judy. "I don't want another dog. We have Zephyr."

"I don't know," said Con. "Maybe we can find someone in town who can adopt him."

"Well, in any case, we have to take him home with us," said Judy.

Raja was perfectly happy to sit in the back seat of the car and wait for Con and Judy to decide what to do with him.

Con and Judy drove Raja back to their house.

"We have to introduce him to Zephyr," said Judy. "How do we do that?"

"We have to do this on neutral ground, so that Zephyr will not feel that his space is being invaded," Con said.

Con and Judy decided that the street outside their house was pretty good as neutral ground. The street was a cul-de-sac, and the house was at the end of the street, so traffic consisted of just a few neighbors, most of whom drove cautiously because their kids often played in the driveways and in the street.

"You hold on to Raja's leash down here, and I'll go up and get Zephyr," Con told Judy.

He ran up the front stairs leading to the front door, grabbed a leash, put it on me, and took me down the stairs to the street.

I could see Judy, holding a strange black dog, another Standard Poodle. The dog was shorter than my 28 inches at the shoulder – perhaps 24 inches at best – and stockier. I am long and thin, and this dog was more compact. The dog had a mass of curly black hair all over his body, matted up in a number of places.

I wasn't sure what was happening, but I am a friendly dog, so I trotted up to say hello. Suddenly, the dog bared his teeth, growled, and lunged at me. I was taken completely aback. Here was Judy holding a vicious dog!

Judy could barely hold Raja. He had learned that the best defense was an offense, and any time he saw a dog he didn't know, he attacked first, on the assumption that the other dog would attack him. He saw me as a threat, not realizing that I wouldn't hurt a fly, much less another dog.

"Con, get Zephyr out of here!" yelled Judy.

"Come on Zephyr, let's go back in the house," Con said.

After I was safely inside, Con and Judy had a conference about what to do with Raja. It was clearly unacceptable to them to have Raja attack me, but on the other hand there was no place to put Raja except in the house. They spent a long time discussing possibilities until Judy hit on a winning strategy.

"Con, do we still have that baby gate that we bought for Zephyr a long time ago?"

"Sure, I think it's somewhere in the garage."

"What would you think about putting Raja in the kitchen with the baby gate keeping him penned in? He could get used to seeing and smelling Zephyr, but he wouldn't be able to attack him," Judy said.

"I think that's a brilliant plan. I'll go look for the baby gate, while you walk Raja around the street for a few minutes and get him calmed down a bit."

And so the baby gate went up. For several days, Raja spent all of his time hiding under the kitchen table. Then he ventured out for a few minutes at a time. I, of course, was very curious and wanted to make friends, so I would approach the gate, only to back off as Raja would start to snarl and lunge. Fortunately, the gate was very solid, and whenever Con or Judy heard Raja's snarls they would rush toward the gate and whisk me away.

Inside the house, Raja was afraid of Con. Perhaps Con's beard reminded him of a former owner. As soon as Con appeared, Raja would retreat under the table and stay there. Con did not like this situation and spent a considerable amount of time talking to Raja in a happy, high-pitched voice. After several minutes of such happy-talk,

Raja would start to wag his tail, but he still did not trust Con enough to emerge from under the table.

"We'll have to find Raja a good home," Con told Judy.

Raja Escapes

Because Raja was hiding, Judy thought she would make it easier for him by removing the kitchen chairs from under the table and putting them out on the front deck. Con was out running some errands, so she locked me in Con's study, then picked up a chair and moved it outside, being careful to close the front door behind her. She was taking out the last chair when a gust of wind came up, the front door blew open, and she saw a streak of black fur bolting down the stairs to the street.

Judy ran down the stairs, yelling "Raja, Raja!" She had only her nightgown on and a pair of slippers, and the day was cold.

Raja first ran up the street, then got spooked by a distant car. He turned around and ran into a large drainage ditch behind the houses across the street. The ditch is mostly dry and serves to catch rain runoff when storms come up. Beyond the ditch is a stretch of weeds and shrubs, and then a clump of townhouses. On the left is a busy street with lots of traffic, and the drainage ditch goes under the street through a large tunnel big enough for elk and a very occasional bear to walk through.

Oh, no, Judy thought. I have lost the dog. How will I explain all of this to Con? I should have checked to make sure that the door was latched properly.

Judy ran to the lip of the drainage ditch. She could see Raja running toward the townhouses.

"Raja, come back! Raja, please come back!" Judy was yelling frantically.

Raja disappeared into a clump of shrubs.

Judy dissolved into tears. She kept yelling for about half an hour, with no result. Raja had vanished.

She started planning a campaign to get Raja back. First, she thought, she needed to phone Con and get him to come back. They would get into their separate cars and start cruising through the streets of the townhouses. Then they would expand their search to a nearby subdivision, driving slowly and calling Raja's name. Judy started to think about what they could put on fliers that they would post around the neighborhood. Unfortunately, they did not have a picture of Raja, so all they could do was describe him.

Judy got so upset at the prospect of trying to find Raja that she sat down on the cold ground, and started to talk to Raja.

"Raja, I want you to know that you can always have a home with us. Zephyr is a very kind dog, and he's not going to attack you the way that other dogs in your life always attacked you. And Con loves you. If we don't find a good home for you, you can join our family and be with us. Please come back!"

She sat for a while, then started to speak to Raja again.

"Raja, I know that you had a difficult first two years of your life. First, you were bought by some people who thought having a puppy was cute, but when you grew and became less fluffy, they abandoned you in their backyard. Then you were thrust into a dog pack where most of the dogs beat up on you. You've had a hard life. But we won't let you down. If we can't find a good place for you, we will love you as part of our family. Please put your trust in us."

As Judy said that, she felt something wet touch the back of her neck. She turned around, and there was Raja, sitting in back of her, nuzzling her neck. He had decided to come back and trust her.

Judy threw her arms around Raja's neck and said, "Thank you for coming back. I love you."

Raja and Judy both happily went back into the warmth of the house.

RAJA FLIES FIRST CLASS

C on and Judy wanted Raja to have a good home. Con started calling all of his friends in the dog world, trying to find someone who might be willing to take Raja. Everyone already had more dogs than they could handle. However, one lady – Joyce – had heard that an organization that trains guide dogs was looking for poodles, because poodles are very intelligent and relatively easy to train. She called a person in this organization, and the person encouraged her to bring Raja in for evaluation. The problem was, unfortunately, that Raja was 500 miles away from where the evaluation was supposed to take place.

Not one to be daunted by such trifles, Joyce immediately booked a plane ticket for herself and for Raja, first-class. Because Raja was about to interview for a guide dog position, he could fly in the passenger part of the plane, occupying his own seat. This would be a long trip for Raja. First, he had to ride in Joyce's car for about two and a half hours to get to an urban airport, then he had to ride in the plane for about an hour, and then he had another hour in a cab to get to the evaluation site. Joyce was confident that Raja would do well.

The morning of Raja's departure was cold, grey, and misty. Con and Judy were worried about how well Raja would do on his trip. The evening before, they had spent a couple of hours writing a long letter about everything that they knew about Raja's prior history, about how he was abused as a puppy and how he was threatened by other dogs when he lived as part of a pack. They suggested that he should be introduced to other dogs very cautiously, because of his tendency to attack first and ask questions later. Con's evaluation was that Raja would turn out to be a kind, gentle, and loyal dog with proper training and reassurance, but it would take some time for him to trust other people and dogs.

I had mixed feelings about seeing Raja go. On the one hand, I was not very enthusiastic about a dog that snarled and lunged at me every time that I showed up. On the other hand, I could sense that Raja was, at heart, a very kind dog, and I was sure that we could become good friends. I knew that with some love and encouragement, Raja would learn to trust me to never hurt him, and we could have a lot of fun together during those lonely times when both Con and Judy were gone from the house. Seri, too, felt that Raja would be a good addition to our household. Raja was not inclined to chase her or be aggressive toward her, so she was pretty confident that he would fit right in.

The time had come to take Raja to Joyce's house. As Con was getting the back seat of the car ready for him, Judy took Raja into her study, threw her arms around him, and said, "Raja, just remember, if things don't work out for you at the guide dog place, you can come back here and live with us. You are a wonderful dog."

Con loaded Raja into the car and drove off. On the way there, Con told Raja the same thing that Judy had told him – if things didn't work out, he was welcome to come and live with us. Even though Con was not enthusiastic about having another dog and was worried about the amount of time it might take to get Raja to become friends with me, he could sense that Raja was a kind and gentle dog at heart.

Joyce was ready to go when Con and Raja arrived. Her SUV had a wire screen dividing the trunk area from the rest of the car, and Raja jumped into that area without any protest. Con gave Joyce the letter that he and Judy had written about Raja and told Joyce that if there were any problems, to please call him immediately. With that, he crossed his fingers and watched Joyce and Raja drive off, heading to the airport two and a half hours away.

When Con came back, Judy asked, "How did everything go?"

"Just fine. Raja did not protest about going. I hope that everything is going to go well."

"Let's hope so," said Judy.

The phone rang that afternoon. It was Joyce. She reported that Raja had done fine on the way to the airport, had been wonderful at the airport with all the people milling around him, seemed quite confident with crowds of people, had sat in his first-class seat and looked out the window most of the time, and had done well in getting off the plane. Joyce was now going to take a cab to the evaluation site. She was quite impressed with how well Raja did on the trip and did not anticipate any problems.

"I think it's going to be fine. I'm glad that Raja is going to go somewhere where he can help people and put his intelligence to use," said Con.

"I'm glad too. Raja is a wonderful dog, but it would have been difficult with another dog around the house. Zephyr is so bonded to us that he might resent having another dog compete for our affection." said Judy.

Actually, I would have been happy to have another dog around the house. I was quite confident that I had assessed Raja's character accurately, and I didn't think there would be any problems.

I know that problems can arise when another dog is brought in. Con tells me that some of the most serious problems in a household arise when people get another dog, because they feel that their dog is lonely and needs company. Usually, they get a puppy, and for a while, things are wonderful between their older dog and the new dog that they bring in. This begins to change when the new dog starts to get older and starts to reach sexual maturity. If the new dog is a relatively dominant one, he or she begins to compete for dominance with the older dog, to the puzzlement and chagrin of the dog's people. Because they first had their older dog, they lavish attention on that dog more than on the new dog, in part feeling sorry for the older dog as the dominance contests start to escalate with growls and snarls. This infuriates the newer dog. He or she escalates the threats even more, eventually to the point where fights break out. Then the owners call Con and ask him what they can do – they thought that they were doing something good for their older dog, and now, suddenly, they are in the middle of a dog war. Con evaluates the relative dominance levels of the two dogs and often has to tell the owners something that they usually do not want to hear – the new dog is more dominant and has to be treated as such. This means priority of access to food, access to strokes, and access to jumping in the car or going outside. The owners are upset. They love their older dog and feel that their older dog should get more strokes by virtue of being with them the longest. Con has to explain that the dog fights will continue until the dominant dog gets treated in a preferential way. Often the owners express regret at bringing another dog into the house.

Since things seemed to be going well with Raja, Con and Judy decided to go to a late afternoon movie. While they were gone, Joyce left a short message: please call her right away.

When the movie ended, Con and Judy called Joyce.

"Well, it looks like you have Raja to yourselves. He washed out of the evaluation program," said Joyce.

"What happened?" asked Con.

"As soon as we arrived at the evaluation site, they put Raja into a pen with five other dogs. He immediately started to snarl at them, so the evaluation people pulled him out of there and told me that he washed out."

"Didn't they read the letter about Raja's prior history and the need for slowly acquainting him with other dogs?" asked Judy.

"They didn't look at the letter, and in any case I don't think that it would have made any difference, because I doubt that they would have taken the time to work with Raja. They said that they are looking for dogs who already know how to behave around other dogs. I'm bringing Raja back tomorrow. Do you want me to drop him off at your house?" said Joyce.

"I guess so." said Con.

I knew that both Con and Judy were pleased and displeased with this outcome. They knew that Raja had the potential to be a wonderful member of the family. But, they were also worried about how much time it might take to get Raja to the point where he was comfortable with me, and could be left alone with me without attacking me.

As it turned out, as soon as Raja was dropped off, he decided that he was home at last. He greeted me with a friendly wave of his tail and allowed me to go through the dog greeting protocols of sniffing his rear. He enthusiastically greeted Con and Judy, then ran up to the couch, jumped up on a couple of pillows, and went soundly to sleep.

"Looks like we have another dog," said Con.

"I think he has finally come home," said Judy.

Living with Raja

Raja and I enjoying the day on our deck.

Raja settled into the fabric of our life. After he got back from his trip, he never made any move to threaten me, and he was rapidly losing his fear of Con. Most evenings, Con would sit down next to Raja on the couch and stroke his head. At first, Raja would growl tentatively, as if to say, I think this is OK but I still don't trust you entirely yet. Con persisted in the strokes, and gradually Raja settled down and allowed Con to stroke him without producing any growls. At that point, Con switched to putting his arms around Raja and gently talking to him, reassuring him in a high-pitched voice that everything was well and that Con was not in the habit of beating up dogs. Before long, Raja was quite content to have Con hold him.

Judy inadvertently stumbled on the passion of Raja's life. She was playing ball with me, throwing a sheepskin toy for me to catch. I tolerated this game because I knew that it amused Judy, but I went only so far in playing it, catching the ball and bringing it only halfway toward her so that she would have to get up and retrieve it in order to throw it again. No matter how hard she tried to get me to bring the ball right up to her, I refused – it was fun watching her get up each time to get the ball.

During all of this Raja was sitting with a confused look on his face, not understanding what was happening. Judy decided to throw my ball to Raja. The ball went sailing past his head, and I ran to get it. Judy took the ball and threw it to Raja again, and again he did not respond. Clearly, he had no idea what to do with a ball. So Judy patiently took the ball to him, put it in his mouth, and then, by holding on to his collar, brought him over to the sofa where she had been sitting, said, "Drop!" and removed the ball from Raja's mouth. Suddenly he got the principle of the game. He ran away from Judy and stood expectantly, waiting for her to throw. As she threw the ball, he clumsily caught it, brought it back to her, and dropped it at her feet. From that point on, he could play ball all day without tiring. He would take his ball to bed with him, and brought the ball to either Con or Judy the next morning for the first catch of the day.

Con was worried about how we would sort out the issue of dominance. As he pointed out, dogs that come into a new home are typically meek and submissive for a few weeks while they try to figure out how to adapt to their new household, but after they have built up their confidence, they can start to assert themselves. Con was concerned that this would happen with Raja. I am a dominant dog. While I am good-natured, I would not tolerate having another dog challenge me in my own house.

Con watched closely for signs that Raja might be developing dominant traits. But Raja turned out to be a puzzle for Con. Raja liked to go through doors first, a sign of dominance. In fact, Con could get him to come toward the house from any distance if he walked up to a door and pretended that he was going to walk through the doorway. Raja invariable came running so that he could go through the doorway first. He also assumed the position of leader dog on walks, wanting to be out ahead of everyone else, another sign of dominance. He liked to jump into the car first. But in everything else, he deferred to me, to Con, and to Judy. Con always gave me my food first, and Raja never protested. After he started to trust Con, he would lie down, roll over, and present his belly to be rubbed, something that I would never think of doing.

BELIEVING IS SEEING

"Come on dogs, we're going to the lake this morning," Judy announced.

She had just bought a canoe, and her excitement level was high for trying it out. I was excited too. A trip to the lake meant walking around a fairly large pond that was near our house. I loved the smells. The wind brought in delicious odors of half-rotting vegetation, of cottonwood trees, of fragrant growing plants. Other people walked their dogs around the lake, so I had a chance to sample dog odors as well, seeing who happened to be by in the last few days.

Judy loaded her canoe on top of her car, while Con loaded Raja and me into the back seat. Raja was even more excited than I. He loved going around the lake. Usually, Judy and Con walked the two of us, me walking with Judy and Raja walking with Con. Today it would be different. We both were going to walk with Con while Judy paddled her canoe.

Con helped Judy unload her boat and launch it into the water. Quick as a splash, Judy took off paddling toward the far part of the lake. Con snapped expandable leashes to our harnesses, and away we went as well.

We were halfway around the lake when we caught up with Judy. She was perhaps twenty feet away from shore, drifting peacefully.

"Hi!" yelled Con. "How's the canoeing?"

"Just fine," Judy replied.

I looked at Judy and wished I could climb into the canoe with her. I imagined that I was Zephyr the famous sailor, striking out to parts unknown, exploring new landscapes.

As soon as Raja heard Judy's voice, he started to look all around the lake. Where's Judy? I can hear her, but I don't see her. He looked at the canoe several times, but did not seem to recognize her.

Con said, "Raja is looking for you and can't seem to see you."

Judy shouted, "Hi Raja!"

This caused Raja to start looking around even more frantically. He peered intently at a person walking on the other side of the lake, then decided that Judy couldn't be over there, that far away. He looked everywhere but at the canoe.

"Why don't you paddle over to the dock over here, and I'll bring the dogs and we'll see how Raja does," Con said. There was a small dock not more than fifty feet away.

Judy paddled up to the dock while Con brought Raja and me up to the edge. I greeted Judy enthusiastically, and made it clear that I would like to ride in her new canoe.

"Con, Zephyr would like to ride in my canoe," Judy said, although it was clear to everyone that I wanted to be in the canoe.

Ever cautious, Con rejected that idea. "You're still getting the feel of the canoe, and if Zephyr gets excited by seeing a bird or a fish, he could tip you over, and there you would be in the water in the middle of the lake, and we don't have a life jacket for Zephyr," Con said.

"Yes, you're right. We'll have to wait until another time, Zephyr," Judy said.

Raja was plainly confused. He could hear Judy and smell Judy – she was only two feet in front of his nose – but he couldn't see Judy. Even though he was looking right at her, he couldn't see her. Judy inside a canoe did not fit into his mental mindset, and he simply could not believe that she was there. He kept looking around, as if Judy would spring out from behind a bush at any moment, and was plainly puzzled that she sounded so close by.

Judy paddled off, and Con took us around to the other side of the lake, where the main dock and the boat ramp were located.

As we got up to the main dock, Judy came up, prepared to beach her canoe and start the process of dragging it up to the roof of her car.

"Hey, Judy!" yelled Con. "Come up to the dock and see if Raja does any better at recognizing you."

Up came Judy, drifting in within a foot of Raja. She reached out her hand and touched his nose, saying, "Hi Raja." Now Raja was thoroughly confused. He could hear and smell Judy and feel Judy, but plainly he still couldn't see her. Once again his belief system prevented him from actually seeing where she was.

When we got home, I teased Raja. Didn't you see Judy right in front of you? Couldn't you have figured it out? I asked.

Raja was defensive. No, I didn't see Judy. I never saw Judy. Where was she?

Right in front of you, I said.

I don't believe you, Raja responded.

It's true, she was there, I said.

As I continued to tease Raja, he got even more defensive.

If you're so smart, how come you get fooled by the cat sounds? he asked.

What cat sounds?

The cat sounds that Judy makes and you never seem to realize that she is the one making them, Raja replied. According to Raja, Judy sometimes made meowing sounds, and I ran frantically around the house, looking for a cat that must have wandered in. Raja said it was plain as day to him that Judy was meowing, but I couldn't seem to realize that it was Judy making the noises.

Now that he mentioned it, I remembered that I would hear a cat sometimes and run around looking for it, but it was plain as day to me that Judy was not making any cat noises. How could she possibly be making those noises, when everyone knew that meows only come from cats? Raja kept assuring me that it was Judy all along, but I still didn't believe him.

Then we started trading notes about the things we believed in. I believe that fresh water comes out of bathroom taps, and if I stand with my front paws draped over the bathtub, eventually either Con or Judy will come along and turn on the tap, giving me a drink of water that is much fresher than the stale stuff that is in my water bowl. Raja said that he didn't believe that water could come out of a tap and that drinking water could only be found in a bowl. Although I tried to convince him, he was adamant in this belief. I asked, haven't you seen me countless times stand in the bathroom and drink from the tap? No, he replied, I have never seen you do that.

Raja, on the other hand, believed that by lifting up his paw, he could pull down the door lever of a door that is closed, and by moving that paw toward him, he could open the door. As he explained, when Con sometimes puts us into his study and closes the study door to keep us away from something that is going on inside the house, Raja would sit patiently and wait for a while, but if Con was too long in letting us out, he would reach up, grab the door lever, and open the door. I had no recollection of him ever doing that. I do remember that quite often the door miraculously flies open under these circumstances, but I still don't believe that Raja ever had anything to do with it.

I asked Con about this.

"Zephyr, it's all true," said Con. "Judy makes cat noises and you never realize that she is the one who is doing that, Raja really can open doors, and Raja can't seem to realize that water comes out of the tap."

Con went on to speculate that rather than "seeing is believing," that really the old adage should be, "believing is seeing." He started to wax philosophical about how humans fall into the same trait and started to wonder about what sorts of things people couldn't see, even when these things were right in front of them. Ghosts? Strange animals? Bigfoot?

This was a little too scary for me, so I wandered off to my couch to catch a nap. Besides, there was no way that anyone could convince me that people can make noises like a cat.

DOG FRIENDS

Sometimes Con and Judy would go for walks in the woods with their friend Steve. I always looked forward to these walks, because Steve had two dogs – a Jack Russell terrier named Hal, and a Malamute named Midge. Both dogs were my friends. I loved to run around with them, smelling every bush, pretending that we were hunting dogs about the catch an elk. We could do all sorts of doggish things together. I enjoyed their company, and they enjoyed mine.

I can almost hear the skeptical reader start to yell – wait a minute, these are just dogs, how can dogs have friends? All dogs are supposed to like each other because everyone knows that dogs don't have much in the way of feelings and just bumble around playing with whoever happens to be around.

Not so. I like some dogs. Other dogs I wouldn't touch with a ten foot pole. I like being around my friends. I hate being around dogs that I don't like.

I know that it's hard for some people, particularly scientists, to believe this. Con has a friend, a psychologist, who believes that all animals are like robots with no feelings, no awareness, and no consciousness. According to this view, which is very common among psychologists, biologists, and people in various animal-related industries, animals can feel pain, but they certainly can't feel love, joy, sorrow, or regret. They don't know that such emotions exist, not having been blessed with self-awareness. They have a limited form of intelligence, enough to help them use pain to learn how to avoid certain things, but any kind of deeper thought is beyond them.

Because they supposedly lack consciousness and self-awareness, animals can be used by humans for all sorts of tests and experiments that people would cringe at doing to other humans. Because they have no self-awareness, animals can be kept in small pens and later slaughtered (the word scientists use is "sacrificed" – it must make them feel better than a more honest word), because the animals don't know what is happening to them in the first place. I heard about a study in which biologists were blowing up beagles with bombs to study the effects of various explosives on living tissue. The rationale was that these experiments would make it easier to treat human soldiers who were blown up during wars. Many domestic animals destined for consumption by humans at the dinner table are kept in conditions that are too horrible for me to think about.

The irony is that many of these same scientists are strong supporters of the theory of evolution. A basic idea of evolution is the concept of "homology" – certain structures have common evolutionary origins. For example, the arm of a human, the front limb of a cat, and the front limb of a horse have common evolutionary origins and are all called homologous structures. At some point in evolutionary time, these structures all had a common function – running. Based on such homologies, the theory of evolution says that if you come across a series of different animals, all with a similar morphological structure, you should consider as a first approximation that all these animals will have the same function for that morphological structure.

Sounds dense? I've been listening to Con's lectures for too long.

Anyway, most of the mammals have brains similar to those of humans. Is it too much of a stretch to believe that what human brains can do, so can the brains of other mammals? To believe that emotions, self-awareness, intelligence, can be found among many, if not all, mammals? The founder of modern evolutionary theory, Charles Darwin, thought that it was quite possible. Unfortunately, many present-day scientists think that it is quite impossible.

But then, as a dog, I see that this is a result of human arrogance, insecurity, and the need for rationalization. The arrogance comes from the human need to be "special." Humans seem to have an almost pitiful desire to be seen as the lords of all creation. It would be kind of endearing in a way, if it weren't so incredibly destructive to all other species of life on this earth. The insecurity comes from a nagging underlying thought: what if it isn't true that humans are the lords of all creation? What if they are only a little blip on the evolutionary landscape? After all, evolutionary theory tells us that dinosaurs roamed the earth for millions of years before they disappeared, and humans have been around in modern form for a mere quarter of a million years, and even that might be stretching it. And now humans are working very vigorously on becoming extinct, just like the dinosaurs, but faster and in a bigger way.

The need for rationalization comes from the need for humans to portray themselves as the "good guys." All people seem to want others to see them as good and kind, even if they really aren't. Humans are capable of endless self-deception.

Maybe someday scientists will start believing that animals have feelings, can think, and can recognize themselves. I'm not holding my breath.

In the meantime, I just want to have a good time with my friends.

DOG SOULS

On a bright sunny day, I saw Con go over to the closet by the front door and get my harness and leash. Oh boy, terrific, a walk! I had been bored all day, sitting around the house, and now that evening was fast approaching I had decided that both Con and Judy would be either too busy or too tired to take me out.

"Zephyr, today just you and I are going out. Raja isn't feeling well, and he's going to stay home with Judy."

We got into the car, with me sitting in my usual position between the two front seats. Off we went.

"Today we're going to walk along some hills that I've wanted to explore for a long time," Con said.

As far as I was concerned, any place at all was just wonderful.

We came to an area where I had been with Judy, but Con had seldom come here with me. I expected that we would explore a fairly densely wooded site, but instead, Con chose a more open area punctuated by low hills and occasional rocky outcrops.

Much to my disgust, Con decided to keep me on my expandable leash.

"Zephyr, there are jack-rabbits, deer, and antelope out here, and the last thing that I want to do is spend the rest of the afternoon looking for you," Con said in response to my whimper of disapproval when he attached the leash to my harness.

But still, a walk is a walk, even if I can't chase a rabbit along the way!

We started walking toward a low hill that had some trees at its base. I was leading the way, as usual, pretending that I was a pathfinder blazing a trail through unknown wilderness, while Con was looking at rocks on the ground and trying to keep my leash from getting tangled up in various bushes.

After climbing to just about the top of the hill, Con realized that on the other side of us, nearly concealed from our view, was a fairly deep and narrow canyon snaking through the countryside with a ribbon of trees growing on either side of the canyon walls.

Con wanted to look into the canyon from the top of the hill, but at the same time, he wanted to approach the steep canyon wall cautiously since he is always worried about my falling off the edge of canyons, walls, and steep rocks. I, of course, wanted to run right up to the edge of the canyon and look down. Who knows what kinds of animals lurk in steep, narrow canyons? Animals that Zephyr, the mighty hunter, can chase?

We had a minor contest of wills, where Con kept pulling me back and I kept surging forward. Finally, Con said, "Zephyr, don't you know that you can fall off the edge and get killed? It must be at least a five-hundred-foot drop down to the bottom of that canyon. If you slipped and fell, your leash would never hold you, and I probably wouldn't be able to get down there to even find you!"

Fuddy-duddy, I was thinking. What do you think? Do you think I'm stupid enough to go leaping off the side of a five-hundred-foot canyon without a parachute? However, with a parachute, it might be a completely different story....

"No, I don't think you will leap off the edge," said Con, knowing full well what I was thinking. "But I do think that neither you nor I know how stable the rocks are along the edge, and with the best of intentions to stay on the rim, either you or I could dislodge a rock and fall down if we got too close."

Well, I wasn't convinced, but he had the leash, and I didn't, so he got his way and hauled me away from the lip of the canyon.

We started to walk toward another hill that was about a mile away. The sun was starting to get low on the horizon, but the day was still warm, and I still had lots of energy left. Back I went to imagining that I was Zephyr Lewis, exploring new countryside while my faithful assistant, Con Clark, brought up the rear along with the supplies.

The hill was fairly steep when seen at close range. Con put me on a short lead, to make sure that I wouldn't get tangled around a bush or a tree on the way up. Even here, I'm not entirely convinced that he didn't think that I would do something dumb like leap off into space while he was trying to negotiate a tricky path among the rocks leading to the top of the hill.

At the top, the view was fabulous. We were looking east at a vista that ran for thirty or forty miles without a human, house, or road in sight. To our west was the sun, closer to the horizon but still casting a warm glow.

Con decided that he wanted to sit down on a rock and look at the view. Since there weren't any really sheer slopes, he wasn't too worried about my falling off the hill, but he also didn't want me getting tangled up in bushes just as he was in the midst of looking at the view.

"Zephyr, Come! Sit! Stay!"

Oh, well, I thought, there are worse things than sitting at the top of a hill looking at the view. Actually, I liked looking at views. It was just that there were all sorts of other things to do as well. I could smell the very recent scent of a chipmunk, and I wanted to find out where he was hiding. There were bushes to smell all around, to find out if any other rodents might be skulking about.

But Con was adamant, so I went to where he was sitting and sat down next to his leg, hoping that at least he would stroke my head as a consolation prize for giving up my exploring.

We sat there for a while. Con was not interested in stroking my head, immersing himself totally in the view.

Just as I was getting completely bored, we both saw something in the distance. A huge golden eagle jumped into the air and started to flap his wings at a tree near a rock outcrop perhaps a quarter of a mile away. Then, finding a thermal, he started to circle in the air, straining to gain height. As he circled, the thermal brought him closer and closer to us, until he was finally circling practically over our heads, slowly moving off toward the setting sun.

I jumped to my feet and leaped up into the air.

"Zephyr, you're not a bird! You can't fly," said Con in his tolerant, superior tone of voice. "Settle down and just watch the eagle."

He had missed the point. I knew I wasn't a bird and couldn't fly. But that didn't stop me from wanting to fly. At that moment, I wanted to leap into the air and soar, spread my wings, and fly into the sun. I wanted to fly around the earth, boundless and free, swooping with joy as the wind caressed my body. Just because I knew that I was a dog and couldn't do that didn't stop me from wanting to do it.

There was something spiritual about watching that bird soar. My soul wanted to go and join that bird on its journey. Even humans feel this now and again as they watch birds fly. There is a human myth, Greek I believe, about a man named Icarus who fashioned wings out of wax, flew too close to the sun, and plunged to his death when the wax melted. Human moralists make this into a parable of how you are supposed to know your limits and not get above yourself, so to speak. I think they miss the point too. I think it is a parable about the soul's journey toward the light, toward freedom from earthbound restrictions that keep our sights set so close in front of us. We animals get caught up in our day-to-day lives, just like humans do. But much more than humans, we can let our souls run free, admiring the mystery and wonder of the world we live in.

The Final Chapter

As I got older, I started to develop a heart murmur. Con and Judy took me to the vet, who explained that there was nothing that could be done except to give me pills that would make me feel better. I started a routine of getting two pills in the morning and one pill at night.

At first, I resisted the prospect of having pills shoved down my throat. It wasn't very dignified, and the pills tasted bad. I would pretend that I had swallowed the pills but instead, would hide them under my tongue until I could get to someplace where I could spit them out without anyone noticing. This made my heart murmur worse, but at least I didn't have to swallow any bad-tasting stuff. For a dog who savored his food, swallowing pills was not on my list of priorities.

Eventually, Con caught on.

"Look, Judy, the dog is being sneaky about his pills. He is spitting them out when he thinks we aren't looking."

"We are going to have to figure out how to make it an enjoyable experience for him," said Judy.

"Do you have any suggestions?"

"Well, one possibility is to give him treats after he swallows the pills. We could open up his mouth, put the pills at the back of his tongue, and then give him a morsel of food that he likes, both to reward him and to make sure that he actually swallows the pills."

"All right, let's try it," said Con.

Judy went and got some of my favorite treats, little cubes that had a liver flavor. I loved eating these and could eat the whole box if Con and Judy were to let me. She pried open my mouth, inserted the pills, closed my mouth, and blew gently on my nose, causing a swallowing reflex. Then she extended her hand and offered me a couple of treats. Oh, heaven! Suddenly, the pills did not taste bad at all.

This became a routine. Eventually, I got so used to it that as soon as Con or Judy would get one of the pill bottles, I would walk up to them and open up my mouth. Anything for a treat!

Con and Judy breathed a sigh of relief.

However, the progress of my heart disease started to make me feel nauseated, or perhaps it was the pills. I started to lose my appetite for the foods that I normally liked to eat. Con and Judy were worried.

"He has to eat. What are we going to feed him?" Judy asked.

"I think we are just going to have to try different foods and see if there is anything that he will be willing to eat," Con said.

So Con and Judy embarked on a series of attempts to get me to eat with the relish and enjoyment that I once had for food. They tried buying expensive dog food in cans. I would eat that food for a couple of days, and then the nausea would come back, and I would lose my taste for it. At first, Con would buy cans of food in larger quantities, because that was cheaper than buying individual cans. But eventually, we started piling up a variety of cans of food that I would not eat.

An unintended recipient of this effort was Raja. Up until then, he was quite content to eat a premium brand of dry dog food. He was happy to lie down next to his food bowl and leisurely munch his kibbles. But Con pointed out that they couldn't feed me one kind of food and Raja another, so Raja got whatever I was offered. Since much of the time I would turn away from my food bowl after a few bites, Raja tried to finish the food in my bowl as well as in his own, particularly if Con was slow about picking up my bowl. Raja started getting somewhat plump.

As I rejected more and more food, Con and Judy became frantic. After one episode in which my heart raced for a couple of days and I felt terrible, I stopped eating entirely. Judy was afraid that I would starve to death.

Because they didn't want to leave me alone and there was nothing she wanted to eat in the house, Judy sent Con off to a fast-food restaurant to bring back some sandwiches. On a whim, Con bought a roast beef sandwich for me to see if I would eat it. He came back holding a bag that smelled delicious.

The smell of the roast-beef sandwich roused me, and I got up and ate it with great enjoyment. So started days of Con or Judy going to the fast-food restaurant and ordering several roast-beef sandwiches because, of course, Raja had to have his share. The sandwiches got me through a rough spot with my health, and eventually I started having more interest in food again.

Con had read that a raw meat diet might help restore sick dogs, so Judy bought New Zealand leg of lamb and fed that to me. That worked quite well for a while, supplemented with an occasional roast beef sandwich. Raja and I were swallowing a large share of the family food budget.

But the heart murmur progressed to congenital heart disease, and the vet said that there was no hope for recovery. He said that it was just a matter of time before my organs would quit functioning.

Con and Judy were distraught. Somehow they thought that if they could feed me the right diet, if they could give me the right pills, if they could give me enough love, I would live forever.

But all things have to come to an end. I got weaker and weaker. It became a huge effort to go outside to pee and poop. Many days, either Con or Judy would carry me outside, stand me up so I could pee, and then carry me back into the house. While I still loved to ride in the car, it became much more difficult for me to stand up or sit on the car seat, and I would end up lying on the seat, unable to see the world outside that I enjoyed so much.

And so I realized that the time had come for me to leave my friends that I had loved throughout my life, and start a new adventure. I hope they will be all right without me to take care of them. But my life is complete. I have loved. I have been loved. It is enough. And with this I leave.

Epilogue

On a sunny summer morning, Zephyr asked to be let outside to pee. Con carried him out and set him on his unsteady, wobbly legs. Zephyr peed and then spent half an hour standing in the sunshine, sniffing in all directions, cocking his head to listen to the birds singing and the distant yelp of a coyote. The wind gently ruffled his ears. Zephyr's tail was wagging, as it always was, regardless of whether he was feeling good or feeling bad. It was his eternal optimism. If he was feeling good, then his tail wagged in gratitude for the wonderful feeling. If he was feeling bad, then his tail wagged in the hope that soon things would be better.

Finally, Con brought Zephyr inside, concerned that he was getting chilled in the cool morning air. Con carried Zephyr into the kitchen and set him down, thinking that he might be hungry. Instead, Zephyr's legs collapsed, and he fell spread-eagle on the floor. Con then carried him to the couch in the living room, where Zephyr appeared to go into a deep sleep. Everyone gathered around him. Seri jumped up on the arm of the couch. Raja sat on the floor just below him. Con and Judy sat on either side of him, stroking his silky apricot fur. Zephyr opened one eye and moved his head so that he could look carefully at everyone in turn, Judy and Con, Seri and Raja, gave a deep sigh and died.

He is greatly missed by all of his friends.

***

Dear readers, if you've recently finished reading this book and it has captivated your imagination or left you thinking about its content long after you turned the final page, I urge you to take a moment to share your thoughts by leaving a review. Your reviews are not only invaluable, but they also play a crucial role in helping other readers discover this book. Whether it's on Amazon, Goodreads, or any other platform, your feedback contributes to a book's visibility and success.

Remember, the more reviews a book receives, the more likely it is to gain traction and find its way into the hands of eager readers. So, let your voice be heard and help shine a spotlight on this book. Your review could be the key to unlocking a new world of reading for someone else.

About the Author

T his book is a collaboration between Zephyr and Con Slobod-chikoff. Zephyr lived through all of the stories described here, while Con dutifully took notes. Con was the scribe for Zephyr's tale of his life.

Con Slobodchikoff is Professor Emeritus of Biology at Northern Arizona University, author of *Chasing Doctor Dolittle: Learning the Language of Animals; How to Talk to Your Dog: You and Your Dog Will Be Happier Once You Learn How to Understand Each Other!;* and is the lead author of *Prairie Dogs: Communication and Community in an Animal Society.*

He has been featured in a variety of news media articles and interviews, including magazines such as *Smithsonian Magazine, National Geographic, Discover Magazine, People Magazine, Reader's Digest*, and *Boy's Life*; radio interviews such as "Radiolab", NPR's "All Things Considered", and NPR Flagstaff, Phoenix, Santa Fe, Idaho, and Colorado; on television on *NBC Dateline, ABC World News with Peter Jennings, CNN, Country Canada, Quantum* (Australia), *Tierzeit* (Belgian-German TV), Turner Broadcasting, and Brixen Productions (Discovery Channel); and in newspapers such as the *LA Times, Boston Globe, Denver Post, Arizona Republic, Arizona Daily Sun, Arizona Daily Star, Washington Post*, and the *New York Times*. A joint production by BBC and Animal Planet did a one-hour documentary of his work, shown in 2010 by BBC TV in Europe and in 2011 on Animal Planet as part of the Mutual of Omaha Wild Kingdom series.

Con has written or co-written some 100 scientific papers and popular articles on animal language, animal behavior, and evolution. He has also edited three books on these topics.

Con also writes or co-writes several blogs, including Reconnect With Nature Blog (www.reconnectwithnatureblog.com), the Dog

Behavior Blog (www.dogbehaviorblog.com), and the Dr Con page on Facebook (www.facebook.com/doctor.con).

His website is: www.conslobodchikoff.com.

Con has a B.S. and a Ph.D. degree from the University of California, Berkeley.

Acknowledgments

Thanks go to my wife, Dr. Judy Kiriazis, who was instrumental in the education of Zephyr, and to Sally Anderson for her extensive editorial review. Thanks also go to all of the animals that I have observed and interacted with over the years — they have taught me a lot about animal behavior.

www.ingramcontent.com/pod-product-compliance
Lightning Source LLC
Chambersburg PA
CBHW070718130626
46553CB00005B/2052